Zimbabwe: A New History

> "History will have its say one day — not the history they teach in Brussels, Paris, Washington or the U.N., but the history taught in the countries set free from colonialism and its puppet rulers."
>
> Patrice Lumumba

by G. Seidman, D. Martin, P. Johnson

Consulting editors: S. Gumbo, G.I.S. Mudenge, Q.N. Parsons
Lay out & design: T. Dunn, M. Philips, D. Corbet
Cover: T. Dunn
Maps: T. Wodetzki
Drawings: C. Hodzi

Zimbabwe Publishing House
P.O. Box BW-350, Harare

Zimbabwe Publishing House
P.O. Box BW-350
Harare, Zimbabwe

© G. Seidman, D. Martin, P. Johnson 1982
First published by ZPH 1982
ISBN O 949932 14 O

All rights reserved

Photographs on pages 120 (top and bottom), 123, 125, 129 (top), and 137 by Louise Gubb; on pages 20 (top) and 117 by Tessa Colvin; on page 136 by Neil Libbert; on page 69 by Parade Publications; and on pages 82, 95, 96, 103, 115, and 129 (bottom) by The Herald/Zimbabwe Newspapers. The remainder of the photographs are from the Zimbabwe Ministry of Information and the National Archives of Zimbabwe.

The publisher has made every effort to trace the copyright holders, but if they have inadvertently overlooked any they will be pleased to make the necessary arrangements at the first opportunity.

Printed in Zimbabwe by Zimpak

Zimbabwe: A New History

History for upper primary school

Chapter Outline

INTRODUCTION		1
CHAPTER 1:	The Stone Age	5
CHAPTER 2:	The Early Iron Age	9
CHAPTER 3:	The Beginning of External Trade	13
CHAPTER 4:	Great Zimbabwe	18
CHAPTER 5:	The Mutapa Empire	24
CHAPTER 6:	The Rozvi Empire	30
CHAPTER 7:	Nguni Invaders from the South	36
CHAPTER 8:	Arrival of the Ndebele	41
CHAPTER 9:	Growth of Imperialism	45
CHAPTER 10:	European Occupation	51
CHAPTER 11:	The First Chimurenga	56
CHAPTER 12:	The Settlers Take Control	62
CHAPTER 13:	African Protest Movements	67
CHAPTER 14:	The Settler Colonial State	73
CHAPTER 15:	The Failure of Partnership	77
CHAPTER 16:	Growth of African Nationalism	82
CHAPTER 17.	Formation of ZAPU and ZANU	88
CHAPTER 18:	The Rhodesian Front and UDI	92
CHAPTER 19:	The Armed Struggle	98
CHAPTER 20:	The Pearce Commission and the new ANC	103
CHAPTER 21:	A New Approach to the Struggle	107
CHAPTER 22:	The Portuguese Coup d'Etat and Detente	113
CHAPTER 23:	The War Resumes	118
CHAPTER 24:	The Patriotic Front	123
CHAPTER 25:	Gukurahundi	129
CHAPTER 26:	The Birth of Zimbabwe	134
OTHER BOOKS TO READ		140

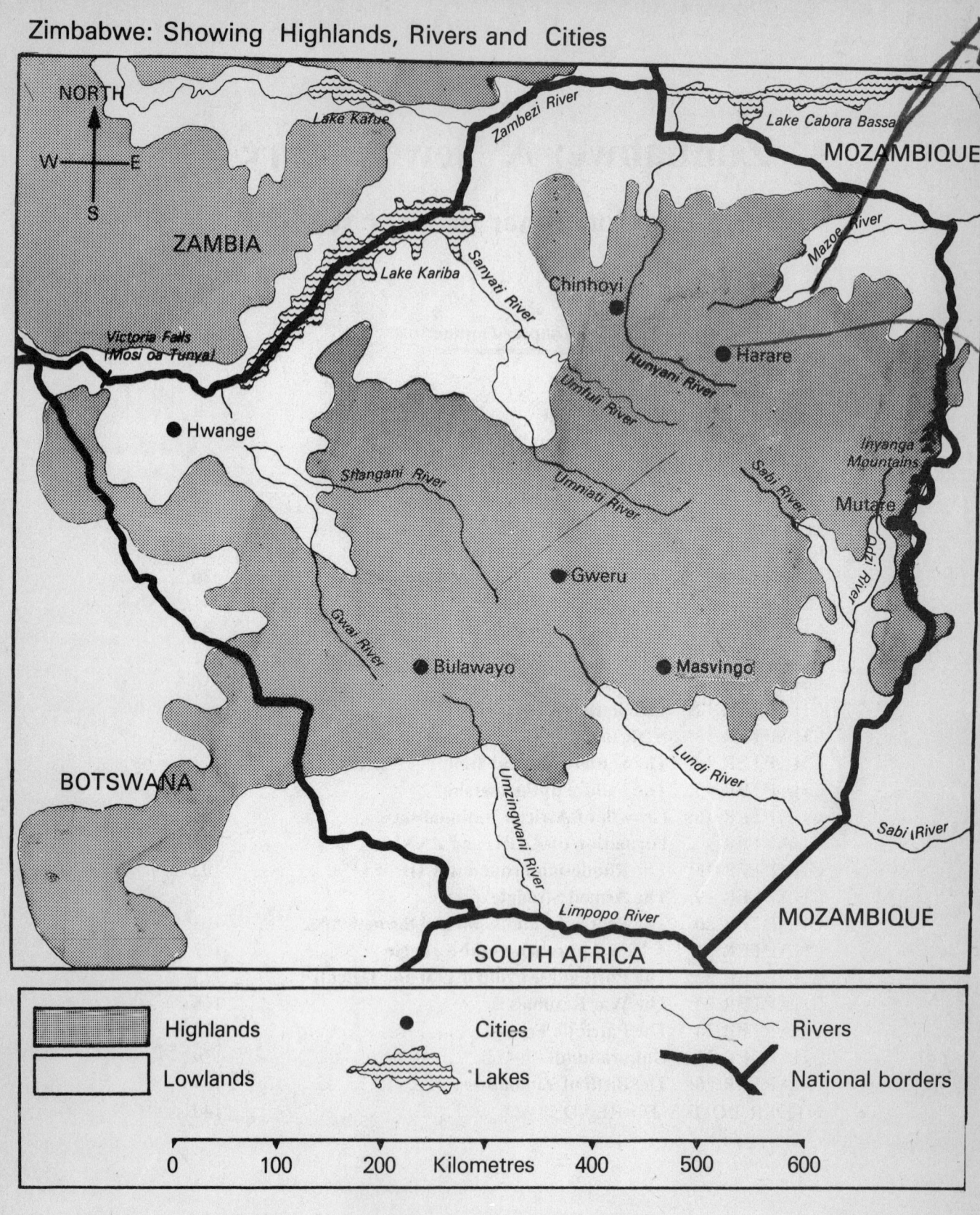

Introduction

History is the story of the past. It tells us how we came to be where we are today. Most of us learn about our family's history from our parents and grandparents. They tell us stories about their lives and the lives of their parents. These stories help us to understand why we live the way we do now. In this book, you can read about the history of Zimbabwe. When you have finished, you should know more about how Zimbabwe developed, and about the lessons we can learn from the past.

Oral History

There are many ways to learn about history. We can learn from books, or from stories passed down through families. Most of what we know of life in **ancient** Zimbabwe comes from these spoken stories, called oral traditions. The people of ancient Zimbabwe did not have a written language. They passed on their history and traditions in the form of stories which the children learned, just as you do now. A family might leave out part of a story that told how they were defeated because they would want their children and grandchildren to think they were strong and brave.

Historians have found that oral, or spoken, traditions also contain a great deal of truth. Sometimes they can check the oral stories with stories written at the same time. For example, they can check oral stories about the Munhumutapa with stories written at the time by Portuguese visitors. The visitors often did not understand what they saw. But it helps our understanding of the past if we have more than one story about the same event.

When writing was not common, people wrote words the way they heard them. People often heard words differently. So the same names may look very different when they are written. For example, the leader of the Mutapa empire is sometimes called the Munhumutapa, Mwenemutapa, or Monomotapa.

Archaeology

Another way to learn about a country's past is archaeology. Archaeology is the **science** of looking at things that people have left behind and learning about their lives from these remains. A person who studies these things is called an archaeologist.

An archaeologist might study the remains of a village where people lived hundreds of years ago. Perhaps the people who lived there found a

Old Portuguese drawing of a Munhumutapa.

better place to live, or their village was destroyed by war or fire. The ruins slowly filled up with soil, and grass grew on top. After some time there might be only a hill where there was once a village. Then, many years later, an archaeologist begins to **excavate** the site. He or she digs out the dirt to find the remains of the village. Objects are found in the ruins which give an idea about the people who once lived there. The archaeologist might find a few old tools, or bits of pottery, or beads or weapons. There might be objects from far away. This would tell the archaeologist that the people who lived there traded with other people. There might be a building which looked like buildings in another place. Then the archaeologist would know that these people were in contact with other people who used the same building style.

Written History

When we want to learn about recent history, we can use books written by Zimbabweans and others. So what we know about the last 100 years is much more detailed than our **knowledge** of ancient times. We can read newspapers, books, diaries and letters written by people who took part in events. It is often possible to talk to these people. This gives us a clearer idea of more recent times. We also have photographs and pictures to show us what places and people looked like.

All of these methods tell us about the past. Oral traditions, written stories, and archaeology. None of them can tell us everything. We are always learning new things about our history. Then we have to change our ideas of what happened. The writing of African history has often been **distorted** to make the people think they had no past until they were "discovered" by Europeans. The stories in most history books, if they were about Africa at all, were about Europeans in Africa. Some of these stories are important parts of our history. It is useful to learn about other parts of the world and find out what other people think. But there are many stories which have been left out of history books.

Historical Twist

The words used in writing a history book can give a different meaning to the same information. The information used or not used can also give a different meaning, just as in oral traditions. For example, a man called Alexander set out to expand the area he controlled in Europe. He fought many wars. The history books written in Europe call him "Alexander the Great". Tshaka did the same thing in Southern Africa. He fought many wars. He fought against the Europeans who came to take his land. Those

David Livingstone was the first European to see the Victoria Falls, and he named them after his queen, Victoria. History books in Europe say he "discovered" the Falls. But this is not true. Africans who lived in the area knew where they were and called them Mosi oa Tunya (the smoke that thunders). Livingstone was taken to the place by his African guides, Susi and Chuma.

same history books call Tshaka a "savage". More recently, before independence in Zimbabwe, the spirit medium of Nehanda was called a "witch" in history books.

Read the stories in this book carefully and ask many questions. Discuss them among yourselves. This book is written for all of the children of Zimbabwe, that you may have a better understanding of where you are today, and that you may learn an important lesson of history — that in unity and **co-operation** there is strength and success.

We have tried to tell this new history in a lively way, by bringing the people alive so you can understand something of their actions at the time. We would be glad to receive your comments, as students and as teachers.

Great Zulu leader, Tshaka.

VOCABULARY

ancient	—	long ago.
science	—	facts put in order and studied to find out what they mean.
excavate	—	dig up.
knowledge	—	what we know.
distorted	—	twisted out of the truth.
co-operation	—	working together.

EXERCISES

Summary
(Copy this passage into your notebook, filling in the blanks.) There are many ways to learn about _____. Some of these are _____, written stories, and _____. _____ means looking at old things to find out about how people lived. There are many lessons to be learned from _____. One of the most important is that there is strength in _____ and _____.

Questions
1. Why can we use more written stories for the last 100 years of Zimbabwe history than for the time before that?
2. How can the telling or writing of history be distorted?

Discuss
Why would history about Africa have been distorted in Europe?

Project
Learn about your own history. Ask your parents and grandparents how your family came to live in your present place. Find out where they lived before, and why they moved. Ask them about their parents' history. Draw a chart showing as many relatives as you know. Start with your mother and father, and their brothers and sisters. Then your grandfather and grandmother, their brothers and sisters, and so on.

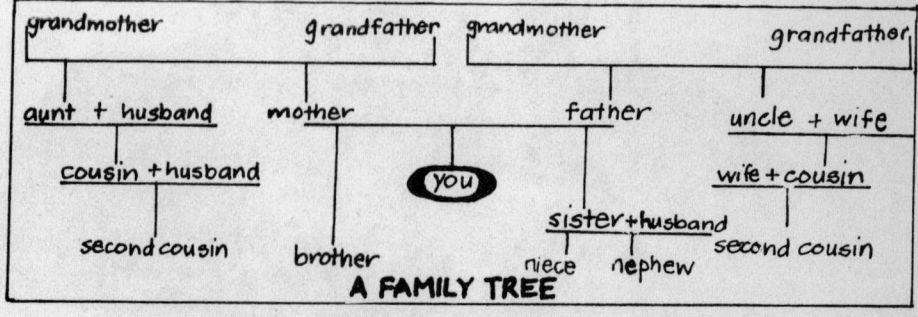

A FAMILY TREE

1 The Stone Age

Stone Age Tools

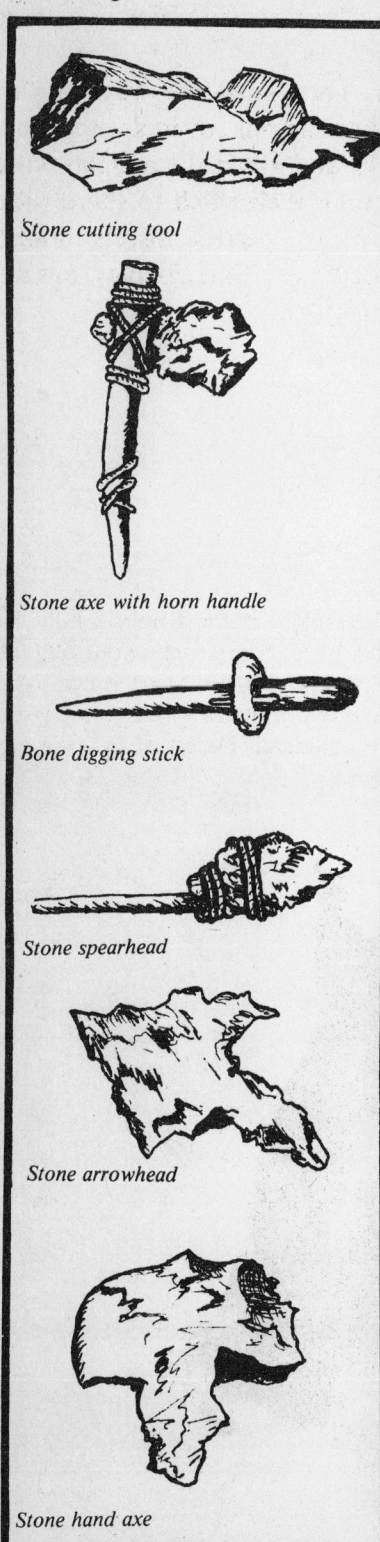

Stone cutting tool

Stone axe with horn handle

Bone digging stick

Stone spearhead

Stone arrowhead

Stone hand axe

The first people who lived on the land between the Limpopo and Zambezi rivers were hunters and gatherers. They hunted wild animals that roamed the land. They gathered wild fruit and plants that grew in the forests and grasslands. They lived more than 50 000 years ago. That is a long time. It is very hard to understand how long it is.

We do not know very much about these early people. We know they did not live in houses. They slept beside big rocks or in caves. They built fires to keep away the animals at night. They did not use metal. They made tools from bone, or by chipping stones to make sharp edges. We say they lived in the Stone Age, because archaeologists have found only stone tools from that time.

Fire and Language

It may seem to us that these early people led very simple lives. But we could not live as well as we do today without some of the things they learned. For example, at first these people did not have fire. Perhaps they got it from a tree that caught fire when it was hit by lightning. Or perhaps a fire started from a spark when they were chipping stones. When they saw how useful fire could be, they learned how to make it themselves. They did this by rubbing sticks together very fast, or by hitting stones to make a spark, then quickly adding dry grass and wood. They also made up a language, so they could talk to each other.

Khoisan

We know much more about the way people lived on the **plateau** between the Limpopo and the Zambezi from about 50 000 years ago. The Khoisan, who are often wrongly called Bushmen, left us more clues about their lives. They painted and cut drawings on rocks or on the walls of caves. Many of these rock paintings still exist in Zimbabwe. They show us how the Khoisan lived, and how they hunted animals.

Way of Life

There are still Khoisan-speaking people living in the Kgalagadi (Kalahari) Desert in Botswana today. Their way of life has changed a lot, but we can learn some things from them about their ancestors of long ago. We know that they lived in small family groups. When they used most of the food that grew wild in one place, they would move to another place. They were not **cultivators**. That means they did not grow their own food. They did not stay very long in one place. So they did not build **permanent** houses. They lived in caves or in shelters made from grass. At that time,

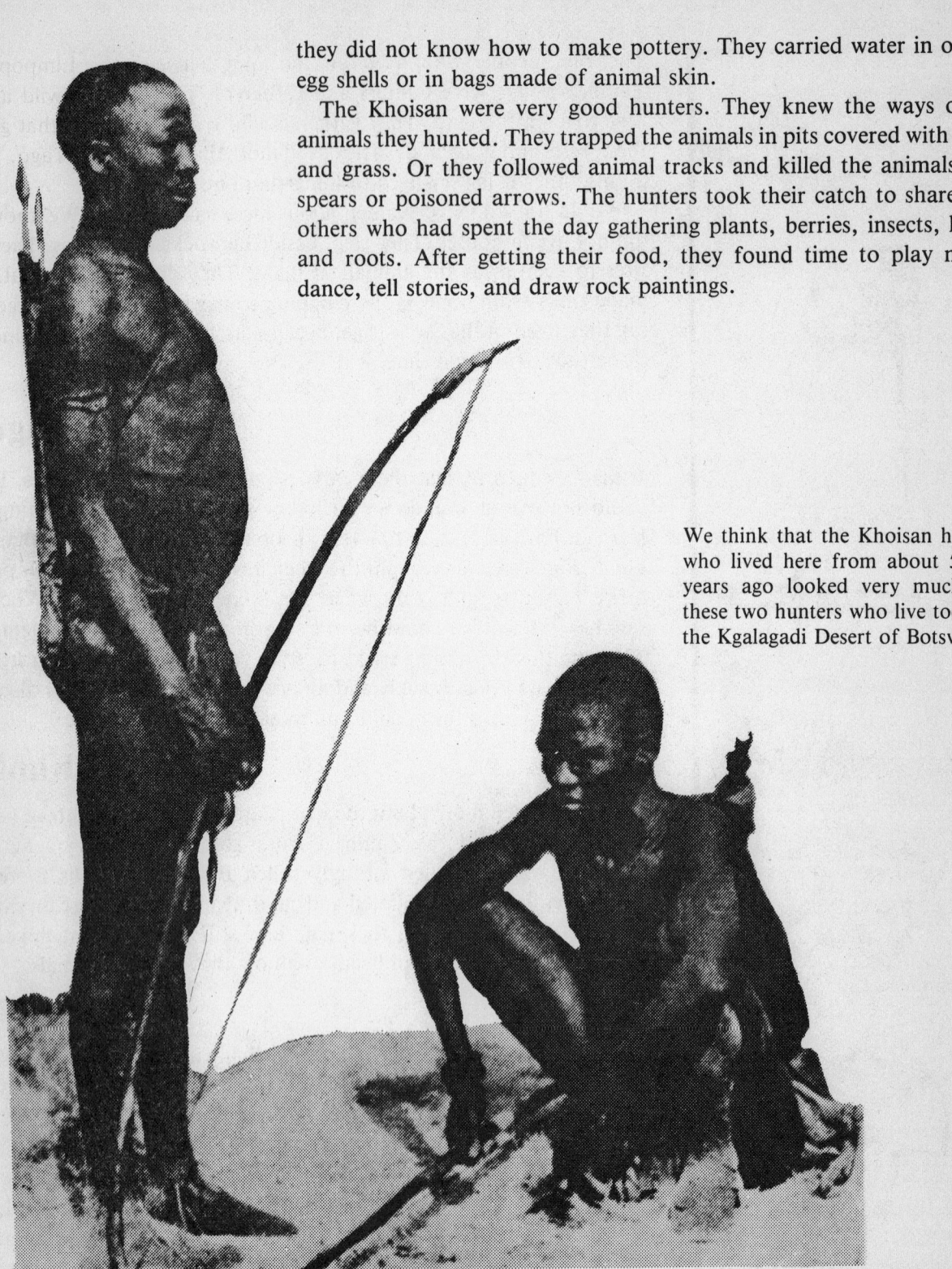

they did not know how to make pottery. They carried water in ostrich egg shells or in bags made of animal skin.

The Khoisan were very good hunters. They knew the ways of the animals they hunted. They trapped the animals in pits covered with wood and grass. Or they followed animal tracks and killed the animals with spears or poisoned arrows. The hunters took their catch to share with others who had spent the day gathering plants, berries, insects, honey and roots. After getting their food, they found time to play music, dance, tell stories, and draw rock paintings.

We think that the Khoisan hunters who lived here from about 50,000 years ago looked very much like these two hunters who live today in the Kgalagadi Desert of Botswana.

Saving for the Future

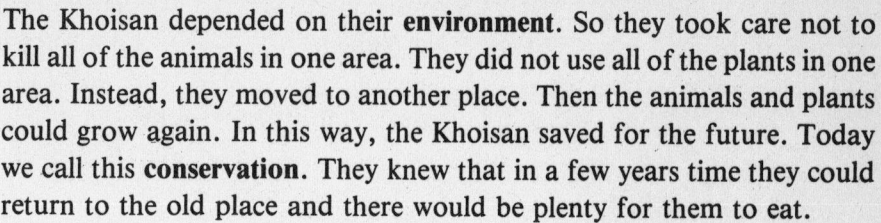

The Khoisan depended on their **environment**. So they took care not to kill all of the animals in one area. They did not use all of the plants in one area. Instead, they moved to another place. Then the animals and plants could grow again. In this way, the Khoisan saved for the future. Today we call this **conservation**. They knew that in a few years time they could return to the old place and there would be plenty for them to eat.

Khoisan rock painting near Harare.

Zimbabwe postage stamps issued in 1982 show different Khoisan rock paintings.

VOCABULARY

plateau	—	an area of high, flat land.
cultivators	—	people who plant and grow their own food.
permanent	—	lasting for a long time.
environment	—	the things around us.
conservation	—	looking after the things around us, such as trees, to prevent loss, waste or damage.

EXERCISES

Summary
(Copy into your notebook filling in the blanks.)
The earliest people who lived here had no _____. They made tools from bone, or by chipping _____. We say they lived in the _____ Age. We know more about the _____ from about 50 000 years ago. Like the earlier people, they got their food by _____ animals and _____ plants. They saved for the future by moving from place to place so the _____ and _____ could grow again.

Questions
1. What did the Khoisan make that we can still see today? What does this tell us about their life?
2. Why did the Khoisan move from place to place? What can we learn from this?
3. Why is conservation still important today?

Discuss
Why did early people make up a language? Why is language important? Think of some of the things you could not do if you could not talk or sing.

Project
Discuss and carry out a project on the conservation of our natural resources. You can fill in dongas with stones and branches to prevent the soil washing away. You can plant grass and trees at your school to stop the soil from blowing away. You can start a tree nursery by planting a few small trees of different kinds.

2 The Early Iron Age

Smelting Furnace

About 2 000 years ago, life began to change on the plateau between the Limpopo and Zambezi rivers. Some people learned how to farm. Some learned how to keep goats and sheep. Some learned how to make pottery. And, most important, some people began to learn how to make tools and weapons from iron. So that time is now called the Early Iron Age.

Iron ore and charcoal put in top of furnace. Air pumped into fire at bottom to melt ore and separate the pure iron.

Way of Life

At first, iron was used only a little. It was used to make light arrowheads and jewellery. Then the use of iron began to spread. More people learned how to find iron **ore.** They dug it out of the ground and crushed it. Other people **smelted** the iron ore in very hot ovens called furnaces. This made it pure. After the iron cooled and got hard again, the village smiths would hammer it into shape. They began to make hoes, axes, spears, and knives.

Working Iron

The people planted millet, sorghum and other crops. They used the iron hoes in their fields. They kept sheep and goats. These were killed at special times such as marriages. They used the spears and knives for cutting meat and hunting wild animals. They could live in one place for a long time without running short of food. So they began to build permanent homes. They used their sharp iron axes to cut wood. They built thatched huts from poles and hard clay (daga). The people grew strong and lived longer, because they had better food and more of it. They had more children, and the population grew. They began to live in larger groups. Farmers moved to new areas when they found that their land was no longer growing enough food. This type of farming is called **shifting cultivation.**

Hammering iron into rough spearhead

Sharpening spearhead

Farm or Move

As some people began to clear land for farming, others had to make a choice. Those who wanted to continue the old way of life could try to defend their hunting grounds or they could move away. It was not easy to

9

Making Pottery

Clay strips made into rough shape

Smoothing the surface

Drying pot in the sun

Baking pot in a fire

defend the hunting grounds with stone weapons. So some groups of Khoisan-speaking people moved away. They moved to the south and west. Some of their **descendants** still today carry on their old way of life in the Kgalagadi Desert. The soil there is too dry for any farmers to want to come and push them off.

Early Trading

People lived peacefully on the plateau for hundreds of years during the Early Iron Age. They grew their food. Most of the other things they needed could be found nearby. They began to trade with each other. A village near a salt **deposit** would trade with another village which was near a good source of iron ore. Or a village could trade sheep and goats for salt or iron.

Bantu Languages

The language began to change. Slowly, over many hundreds of years, a language called Bantu began to spread through eastern and southern Africa. People were moving too. But they moved in small groups and very slowly. Perhaps a group of people would seek better land. Or perhaps one group would split into two. Or perhaps a group of young people would go off looking for adventure. Probably each small group had different reasons.

As each group moved to a new area, their language changed a little. We know that Bantu-speaking people mixed with Khoisan-speaking people because there are words in modern Shona which come from Khoisan words. Some of these are *gomo* which is the word for mountain, *hwai* which means sheep, and *zamu* which is breast. The "clicks" in many of the southern Bantu languages, such as Ndebele, come from Khoisan.

Now there are many different **Bantu languages**. Shona and Ndebele are Bantu langauges. They are related and can be traced back to this time. In the Bantu langauges, the word for people is *bantu* or a similar word. For example, in Shona the word for people is *vanhu*. In Ndebele, the word for people is *abantu*.

Blacksmiths smelting in Charter area, 1944.

Spread of Bantu Languages

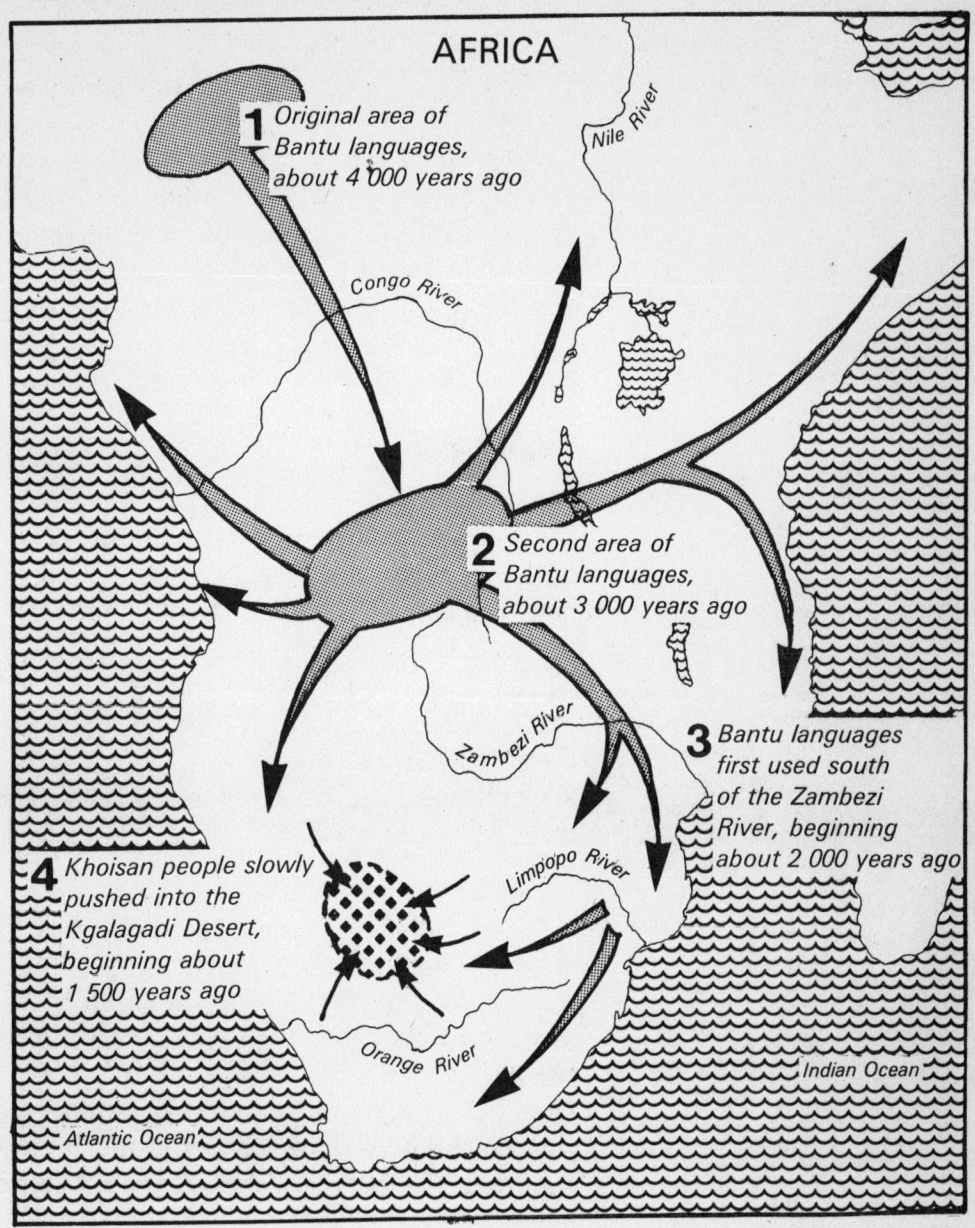

Note: We know that languages in many parts of Africa are related. But we do not know for certain why or how this happened. This map shows one idea of how the languages spread. There are many other ideas, so we should keep on asking questions.

VOCABULARY

ore	— minerals, such as iron, as they are found in the ground, before refining.
smelted	— used heat to melt and seperate the metal from the stone.
shifting cultivation	— growing crops somewhere else for a while so the land in one area can rest.
descendants	— their children and their children's children, and so on.
deposit	— a place where a certain mineral is found, such as salt, gold or iron.
African languages	— a group of related African languages.

EXERCISES

Summary

Life on the plateau began to change. The people learned how to _____, how to keep _____ and _____. They learned how to make _____. Most important, they learned how to use _____ to make _____, _____, _____ and _____. This time is now called the _____ _____ _____. People could live in one place for a long time because they grew their own _____. They built more permanent homes from _____ and _____. They had more children and the _____ grew. The _____ languages spread and changed.

Questions

1. Explain why people could live in one place for a longer time and what effect this had on their lifestyle?
2. How did iron change their way of life?
3. How did the Bantu languages spread and change?

Discuss

Draw a chart in your notebook, like the one below. Write in the spaces in your notebook to show the way of life in the Stone Age and the Early Iron Age. The first one is done for you. Compare this with how you live today.

	Stone Age	Early Iron Age
a. Food	Hunted animals and gathered fruit.	Kept sheep and goats and planted crops.
b. Shelter		
c. Language		

Project

Make a list of crops grown today. Choose some crops from the list and plant the seeds in a school garden. Watch them grow. Remember the plants will have to be weeded and watered.

3 The Beginning of External Trade

About 1 200 years ago, another important change began to take place in the lives of people on the plateau. Men came from Arabia in sailing ships to the east coast of Africa. They came as far south as the area now called Mozambique.

Muslim Traders

These Muslim **merchants** wanted ivory and gold. They built trading centres along the coast, at places like Kilwa and Sofala. The people who lived in these ports became known as "Swahili". This comes from an Arabic word meaning "coastal plains". The Swahili bought ivory, gold and copper from the people who lived inland. They sold these goods to the Muslim merchants. The Swahili middlemen took a share of the goods for doing this. Many of the Swahili people accepted the Muslim religion, Islam. They learned to read and write Arabic. The Swahili culture was greatly influenced by the culture of the Muslim traders.

Arab dhow carrying goods for trading

Sea Trade Routes between Africa & Asia, 1100-1400

Note: On this and other maps the present day borders of Zimbabwe are marked in dashes and surrounded with gray tone. These borders did not exist in early times, but they are marked here so you can locate historic events in relation to where you are now.

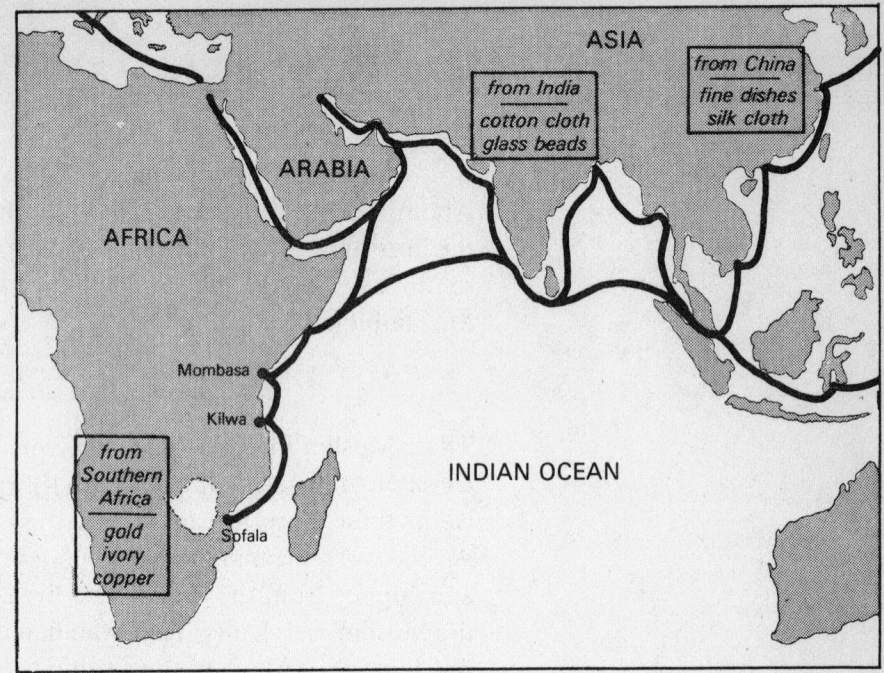

Traders from Asia

Later, men from Asia came to trade along the east coast of Africa. They followed the **monsoon** winds which blow westward from Asia in December and January. They found they could get ivory and gold in return for glass beads and cloth they brought from India and silk from China. In July and August, when the monsoon winds blow in the other direction, they sailed home to sell the gold and ivory in their own lands. This exchange and **distribution** of goods is called **commerce.**

It may be difficult today to understand why gold was exchanged for beads and cloth. But at that time, glass beads were used as jewellery by the people who lived on the plateau, in much the same way as people in other parts of the world used gold as jewellery. The people who lived on the plateau made their own beads from shells. But **imported** glass beads were not common and were given a high value when trading for cattle, grain and tools. The people of the plateau could also make very fine cloth of their own. But they soon found that they could buy more cloth with the gold they mined in a few hours than they could have made themselves in the same length of time. So it was often easier to buy cloth from outside than it was to make it. This is called **importing** goods.

Ivory and Gold

The people who lived inland had many ways of catching elephants, whose tusks are made of ivory. They sometimes dug large pits for the elephants to fall into, just as the Khoisan had done. They sometimes waited in trees until a herd of elephants passed by. Then they speared the animals from above. A brave hunter might attack an elephant with an axe, but this was very dangerous.

The people of the plateau also washed for gold. This means that they scooped sand and gravel from the river beds in shallow pans. They shook the pans until shiny specks of gold appeared. Later, they learned to mine gold, using hoes, picks and shovels. Some people dug down to the gold under the ground. They put the ore into baskets and passed it to other people waiting above. Both men and women were miners. Mining was dangerous work. Often the mines collapsed and crushed people working inside. The people who lived near gold deposits became skilled miners.

Mining Gold

Digging underground for gold

Pulling up gold ore in baskets

Washing for Gold

Elephant showing ivory tusks

Trade Routes

After a lot of ivory or gold was collected, it was carried to the ports on the coast. People walked a long way carrying these goods, through what is now Mozambique. In time, the carriers began to use the same paths again and again. These paths are called trade routes. New ideas travelled along these trade routes. New crops, such as bananas and yams, were brought to Africa by the Asian and Muslim traders. But the new plants did not replace millet as the main food crop.

Carrying ivory and gold to coastal ports.

Later Iron Age

The people who lived on the plateau continued to plant millet, and keep goats and sheep. They began to keep cattle. They made pottery and used iron tools. Small groups of people continued to move around as they had done before, looking for new land. Families grew larger and split up into many units. Some came together in villages under a headman or chief. The chief and the elders made rules. They handled problems over land or cattle or marriages. Many of their customs were similar to those of Shona-speaking people today. We call this period, beginning about 1 000 years ago, the Later Iron Age.

VOCABULARY

merchants	—	traders, especially those doing business with other countries.
monsoon	—	heavy seasonal winds and rain that blow across the Indian Ocean.
distribution	—	sending out.
commerce	—	exchange and distribution of goods.
imported	—	brought from outside (the country).
importing	—	bringing goods from outside (the country).

EXERCISES

Summary

About 1,200 years ago, _____ merchants began coming to the coast in _____ ships. They came as far south as the area now called _____. They built trading centres at _____ and _____. The people who lived in these ports became known as _____. This name came from an Arabic word meaning _____ _____. Many Swahili people accepted the Muslim religion, _____. Then traders came from _____. They followed the _____ winds. They brought _____ and _____ from _____. They brought _____ from _____. They traded this for _____ and _____. This trading is called _____.

Questions
1. The people of the plateau made their own beads and cloth, but they preferred the imported goods. Why was that?
2. What was the importance of trades routes?
3. How is gold mined today? Is it still dangerous work?
4. What other minerals are mined in Zimbabwe today?

Discuss

Should goods be imported when they can be made locally? What does our country import, and why? What does it export?

Project

What can you produce at your school to trade for things you do not have? For example, at the end of the last chapter you were asked to plant a school garden. You could plant some more seeds and make it bigger. You could get a few chickens to raise at school. You could then sell the vegetables and the eggs. The money could be used to start a school library, or to buy more books for the school library.

4 Great Zimbabwe

The name of our country, Zimbabwe, has its origins in the great stone walls that still stand in the south-east near the Mutirikwe River. We know very little about the builders of the walls. Most of what we know is based on archaeology.

The Enclosure *(Imbahuru)* at Great Zimbabwe. This shows the freestanding walls of Zimbabwe-type ruins.

Artifacts

Locally made pottery and **artifacts** found in the area of Great Zimbabwe show that people lived there long before the walls were built. Archaeologists have found pieces of pole-and-daga huts, and animal figures made from clay. Imported pottery and glass beads found in the ruins are dated later, during the time the walls were built, in the 13th and 14th **century.** This shows that the people living there were trading with the merchants you learned about in the last chapter.

Artifacts from Great Zimbabwe

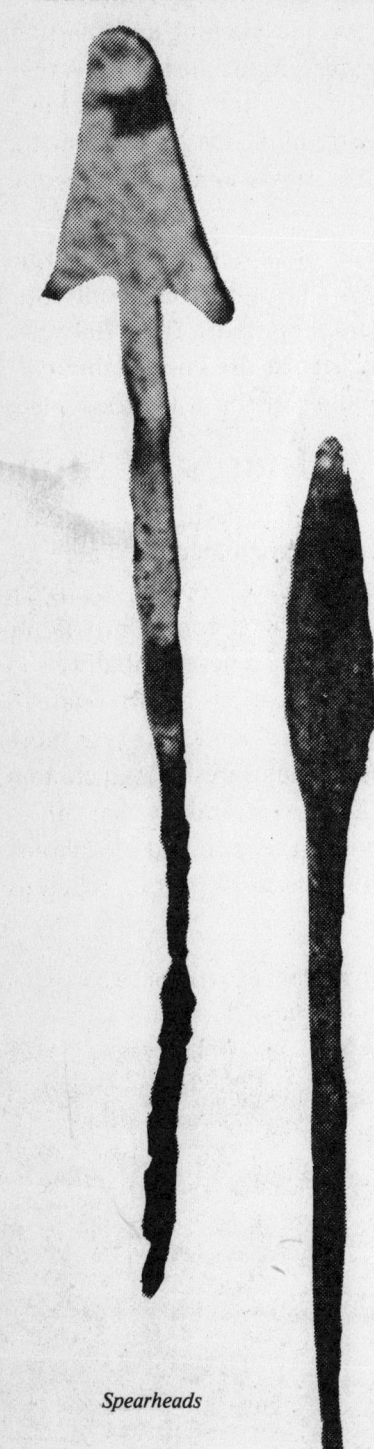

Spearheads

Many objects that tell us about trade have been found at Great Zimbabwe: glass beads, shell beads, bangles and wire made from brass and iron, gold paper, gold beads, coral, copper chains, and many tools made from iron. These objects tell us about **internal** trade, as well as external trade. Gold, copper and iron ore were not mined near Great Zimbabwe. The deposits were to the north and south-west. That means that there was a lot of trade with villages in different areas. Ideas and customs from Great Zimbabwe spread over the plateau.

Glass beads
Gold foil
Wire
Weights

Cattle

The people who lived at Great Zimbabwe grew millet for beer and food, and vegetables for relish. They kept a lot of cattle. They may have washed for gold in the river. More likely they traded cattle and other goods for most of their gold, iron and copper. The nearby valley of the Sabi River could have been a trade route from the gold mines in the south-west to the coastal port of Sofala (in what is now Mozambique). Thus, the people of the area around Great Zimbabwe may have become traders themselves, first trading cattle for gold, then trading the gold for imported goods. But most archaeologists believe the wealth of the area was based on cattle.

Known and Unknown

There are many things we do not know about Great Zimbabwe. Studies in the future may give us more information. We do not know the purpose of the conical tower filled with stones which stands inside the great walls, or the use of several artifacts found there. We do not know the meaning of the chevron pattern (v-shaped) on the outside wall. We do not know how many people lived there. It might have been 5 000 or 10 000.

We know that the site would have looked very different when it was full of daga huts, footpaths, cooking fires, people laughing and chatting, and cocks crowing. We know that the pottery found inside the stone walls is smoother and has many different designs than the rougher pottery found outside the walls. Archaeologists think this means that the rulers lived inside the walls and their relatives, advisers and other people lived outside.

The great stone walls show that it was an organized and **prosperous** society. They show the power of the state. The walls were built from stones, without mortar, yet they are still standing more than 700 years later. This work needed skill and time. It needed organized **labour**. A new method of dating shows that the building of the walls took place over a period of more than 200 years.

Houses of Stone

Zimbabwe means 'houses of stone'. The term has been used since the 16th century to describe the dwelling place of Shona leaders. There are many such **enclosures,** zimbabwe, all over the plateau. None are as big as the one at Great Zimbabwe. Granite was the most common building material, but other stone was used in some places. These zimbabwe do not seem to have been built for defence. Their locations do not relate to mining deposits or trade routes or good agricultural land. The sites more often relate to grazing lands for cattle. Most enclosures would contain dwelling places for only a few people. So it does seem likely that others lived outside the walls. They may have provided the food and the labour. Oral traditions say the hill at Great Zimbabwe was an important religious centre.

Conical Tower in Great Enclosure

Chevron pattern on wall of Great Enclosure.

Zimbabwe Birds

Soapstone carvings have been found at Great Zimbabwe and not at other, smaller sites. Among the many carvings are soapstone birds. At least six of these once stood in an enclosure at the top of the hill. Some were found in the valley. The birds were cut down by early European **prospectors** about 100 years ago. Most of them were taken out of the country. Five complete birds and part of another were returned after Independence in 1980. One of these birds is now the national symbol of Zimbabwe. A picture of one of the birds is on the flag, and also on the money. A picture of Great Zimbabwe is on the one dollar coins.

Damage by Prospectors

One problem in looking for information about the origins of Great Zimbabwe is the damage done by early European prospectors. They broke many objects and carried away others. They wanted the gold, copper and brass to sell in Europe. European settlers who dug later did even more damage. And they claimed that Great Zimbabwe was built by Europeans, or Arabs, or Phoenicians from the north coast of Africa. Now we know that Great Zimbabwe was built by Shona-speaking people of the later Iron Age, in the 13th and 14th century.

Abandoned

Archaeological sites in Kenya and Tanzania have given us a lot of information about Indian Ocean trade. This shows that trade was taken over by the Portuguese from the 16th century. No objects from this period have been found at Great Zimbabwe. So archaeologists believe that the state at Great Zimbabwe came to an end during the 15th century. The town was burnt and the site abandoned. It was common then for a town to be burnt when the ruler left.

We do not know exactly when or why the people left Great Zimbabwe. They may have moved to new land, or perhaps there was an outbreak of disease. But it seems more likely that the population grew too large and used up all of the resources. The population grew and the people stayed in one place. The natural resources, such as timber for firewood, soil for growing food, grazing land for the cattle and wild animals, were used without rest. A minor drought or crop failure could have caused major problems.

Zimbabwe flag
Soapstone carvings
Zimbabwe coin

VOCABULARY

artifacts — objects made by people.

century — the counting of centuries is a bit confusing. For example, we live in the 20th century but we call the year 19.... In the same way, the 13th century means the 1200s. This is so because Christians a long time ago began counting from the year they marked as the birth of Christ. They called the years before that BC (Before Christ). They called the years after that AD (Anno Domini, that means the "year of our Lord" in Latin). They started counting AD 1. That was the beginning of the first century. When they got to 100 that was the start of the 2nd century, and so on.

internal — inside, in this case inside the country. External trade would come from outside (the country).

prosperous — successful.

labour — work, or the people who do work, workers.

enclosures — walls or fences around something, in this case stone walls around huts.

prospectors — people who search for gold and other objects of value.

EXERCISES

Summary

Many objects that tell us about trade have been found at Great Zimbabwe. Some of these are _____ _____, _____, and _____. These tell us about _____ trade, as well as _____ trade. It was through trade that _____ and _____ from Great Zimbabwe spread all over the plateau. We know that the people who lived at Great Zimbabwe kept many _____. We do not know the meaning of the _____ pattern on the outside wall. Zimbabwe means _____ _____ _____.

Questions

1. Whom do we think lived inside the stone walls at Great Zimbabwe? And who lived outside?
2. How do we know that it was an organised and prosperous society?
3. Why was the city abandoned?

There are many smaller zimbabwe in other parts of the country. This shows part of a zimbabwe at Inyanga

Discuss
Why is organization and co-operation important in building a strong and prosperous society?
Project
If there is a zimbabwe near you, perhaps the class can go to see it. If there is a museum nearby, visit the museum and find out what information they have. If your school is building new classrooms you can find out how a wall is made today. You can learn more by helping to build it.

Great Zimbabwe: Showing the Hill in front, with The Valley and The Great Enclosure behind.

5 The Mutapa Empire

Early in the 15th century, a man called Mutota moved north to the Zambezi valley. Some oral traditions say he came from Great Zimbabwe. He settled in the Dande area, ruling over the Tonga and Tavara people who lived there. Written stories say the place was chosen because of nearby villages which had ores and salt to trade. Oral traditions agree that Mutota migrated, or moved, in search of salt deposits. His son, Matope, became the first Munhumutapa, the ruler of Mutapa.

Way of Life

The Shona-speaking rulers of the Mutapa **empire** governed a large area between the Tsatse, Mazoe and Zambezi rivers. The people who lived in that area paid **tribute** to the Munhumutapa with grain, gold, ivory, or whatever they had. In times of famine, the Munhumutapa gave grain to the people so they would not go hungry. Otherwise, the tribute added to the wealth of his court. The Munhumutapa had many wives and many court officials to carry out his business. Some of the wives also acted as officials, greeting visitors and taking their business to the Munhumutapa. Members of the court lived very well. They wore fine cloth. They had beautiful hairstyles and lots of jewellery. The other people dressed in rougher cloth or skin. The Munhumutapa had great power over his people and some traditions say he was treated like a god.

This method of crushing grain has been used for centuries.

The armies of the Mutapa empire travelled over long distances. They were armed with spears, clubs, axes and bows. They attacked subjects who did not pay tribute to their leader. They attacked by surrounding their enemy. Their defence was their long, thin wooden shields. They pushed the shields into the ground to form a wall around themselves.

The people of the Mutapa empire worshipped one god, called Mwari. He spoke through the spirits of the ancestors. The Munhumutapa and his people listened carefully to the spirit mediums. They had special days to honour the ancestors. Then the people celebrated with music, dancing and feasting.

The people of the Mutapa empire had the same language, customs and culture as their relatives at Great Zimbabwe. But they did not use the name Shona in those days. They called their language Karanga. The word Shona was not used until the 19th century. It is believed to be a term first used by the Ndebele to describe the people who lived to the west, *entshonalanga*. The term Shona is now used to describe many related languages in Zimbabwe, one of which is Karanga.

Members of the Munhumutapa's court might have worn their hair like this.

Coming of the Portuguese

A Portuguese captain named Vasco da Gama sailed three ships around the coast of Africa in 1497-8. He was the first person to do this. Da Gama was on his way to India where he hoped to buy spices, gold, and other goods to sell in Europe. He landed at the coast of what is now Mozambique, and at Malindi, in what is now Kenya. He saw how rich many Muslim traders had become from the gold trade.

Da Gama returned to Portugal and told his king what he had learned. Some Portuguese merchants came to the coast of present day Mozambique after 1505. They hoped to get rich by taking gold and ivory from Africa to Europe. Others who came were criminals who were freed from jail in Portugal if they promised to settle in Africa. Some were Christian missionaries.

When the Portuguese arrived, they heard about the great wealth of the Munhumutapa and his gold mines. They sent people inland. From about 1540, a small group of Portuguese men lived at the Munhumutapa's court. At that time the court was at Musapa in the land of Mutapa, or Mukaranga as it was known then. A few Muslim traders also stayed at the court. The Muslim and Portuguese traders had to obey the orders of the Munhumutapa. They paid a kind of tax, or *curva*, in cloth in exchange for being allowed to trade there.

Vasco da Gama, the Portuguese explorer who charted the sea route around Africa to Asia.

Vasco da Gama's Route around Africa, 1497-98

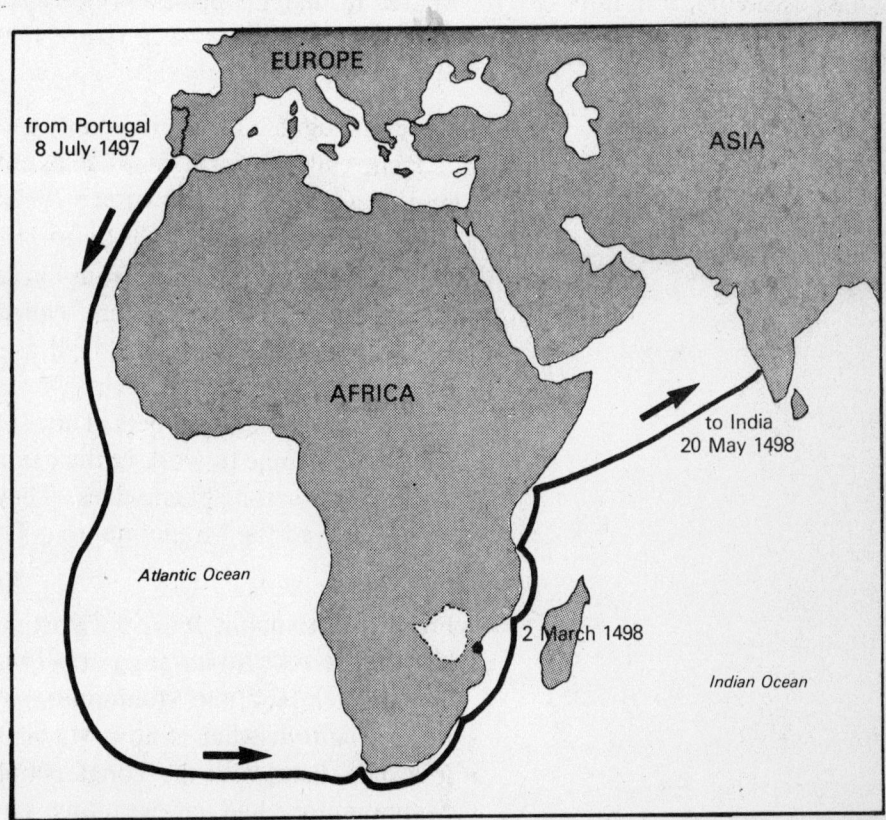

Silveira

In 1560, a Portuguese missionary named Goncalo da Silveira went to live at the court of the Munhumutapa Nogomo Makunzagutu. Silveira converted some of the people to Christianity, including the Munhumutapa's mother, and then the Munhumutapa. But the Munhumutapa ordered his **execution** in 1561. The Portuguese traders said this was because the Muslim traders were afraid of Silveira's power and had told the Munhumutapa that he was a spy who was planning an attack.

When the news of Silveira's death reached the Portuguese king, he decided to invade the Munhumutapa's land and take over the gold mines. In 1570, Francisco Barreto led a large Portuguese army into the Mutapa area. They did not know the area. They wore heavy metal armour. They had cannons and very simple guns. They could not defeat the people of Mutapa. After two years of fighting, many of the invaders had been killed or had died from sickness.

For the next 35 years there was peace in Mutapa, and the Portuguese traded with the people there. But in 1607, the Munhumutapa Gatsi Rusere asked the Portuguese to help him fight against another man who wanted to take his place as ruler. Gatsi Rusere gave the Portuguese the silver mines at Chikova in return for their help.

Execution of Silveira, as drawn by a Portuguese artist. The people and the buildings do not look African.

Prazos and Prazeros

More Portuguese men arrived and moved inland. They took large areas of land, called *prazos,* in what is now Mozambique. Each Portuguese land-owner trained his own private army of Africans.

In 1628, the son of Gatsi Rusere, Munhumutapa Kapararidze, tried to send the Portuguese away from his land. But there was disunity among his people. The *prazo*-owners, called *prazeros,* fought against him to make Mavura the Munhumutapa. Mavura gave the *prazeros* even more power in return for their help. The *prazeros* became very strong. They fought against nearby chiefs. They stole their land and their cattle. They forced the people to work in their mines and their fields. These *prazeros* also fought among themselves. They were wild and lawless. They no longer obeyed the Munhumutapa. They had their own power.

Move to Mozambique

From 1628 to about 1667, the Portuguese *prazeros* took more and more land in the rich Mukaranga area. Mavura and his sons could not stop them. After 1667, the Munhumutapa Mukombwe moved with his court to new land in what is now Mozambique. He built a new state in the lowlands there, with the Tonga people. By this time, the subjects of the Munhumutapa had new weapons. They had guns which they had bought or been given as tribute by coastal traders. Mukombwe brought new chiefs to power and restored order in the area he ruled, which was much smaller than before. He did not force the people to pay a lot of tribute. He treated the chiefs as his friends. They helped him to defend the area from more invasions. They had learned that they were stronger when they worked together.

Disunity and Decline

The son of Mukombwe became the next Munhumutapa. His name was Nyamende Mhande. The Portuguese missionaries converted him to Christianity and gave him a new name, Dom Pedro. In 1692, he was overthrown by Nyakunembiri, with the help of the first Rozvi Changamire, Dombo (next chapter).

A Mutapa state continued to exist in the Zambezi valley, in the Dande and Chidima areas, until the end of the 19th century. But the land was very poor and the people were poor. The Munhumutapa had very little power. The Portuguese often **exaggerated** the power of the Munhumutapa, so they could claim to be helping the ruler of the whole plateau. But as we shall see in the next chapter, the interior was now ruled by the Rozvi under the Changamire Dombo. Dombo had pushed the Portuguese off the plateau and created the **boundaries** of present-day Zimbabwe.

Working Gold

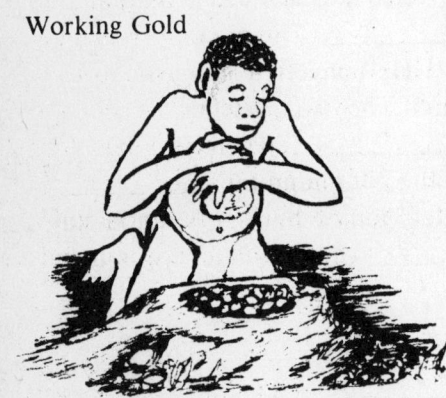

Crushing gold ore

Melting and separating gold

Shaping gold into jewellery

VOCABULARY

empire — group of states under one ruler
tribute — goods paid to a ruler in return for safety.
execution. — punishment by death.
invade — enter with armed forces in order to attack.
exaggerated — claimed it was bigger than it really was.
boundaries — borders.

EXERCISES

Summary

_____ merchants came to the coast of what is now _____ in about _____. They heard about the wealth of the inland _____ mines. Some went inland and lived at the court of the _____ with the other _____ traders. This was at Mutapa, in the land of _____, known as _____. A missionary named _____ went to live at the court. He converted many people to _____. But other people thought he was getting too much _____. He was executed in _____. Then the king of _____ sent a big army. Later, the Munhumutapa _____ moved away to the lowlands. New chiefs joined him. A Mutapa state continued until the end of the _____ century, but it was much _____ and _____.

Questions

1. Who was Mutota? Where did he come from, and why?
2. How did the language come to be called Shona, and when?
3. Why was Barreto's army not able to defeat the people of Mutapa?
4. Why were the *prazeros* able to force Mavura to do what they wanted?
5. Why did Mukombwe move?

Discuss

When the people of Mutapa were divided they were defeated. But when they worked together they were able to defeat the Portuguese who were themselves divided. Discuss how and why unity made them stronger. How does this apply today?

Project

As a class, or in group of about ten, act out a play of Mavura's problem with the Portuguese. Here are some suggestions.

Scene 1: Mavura argues with Kapararidze over who should be Munhumutapa. They are divided and so they are weak.

Scene 2: Kapararidze starts to argue with the Portuguese living at his court, demanding they pay the **curva**. The Portuguese do not want to pay. They are united so they are strong.

Scene 3: The Portuguese make a deal with Mavura. If he will promise to let them have more land and mines, they will help him defeat Kapararidze.

Scene 4: Kaparidze is defeated in battle, and Mavura is made Munhumutapa.

The Mutapa Empire and the Portuguese invasion, 1450/1650

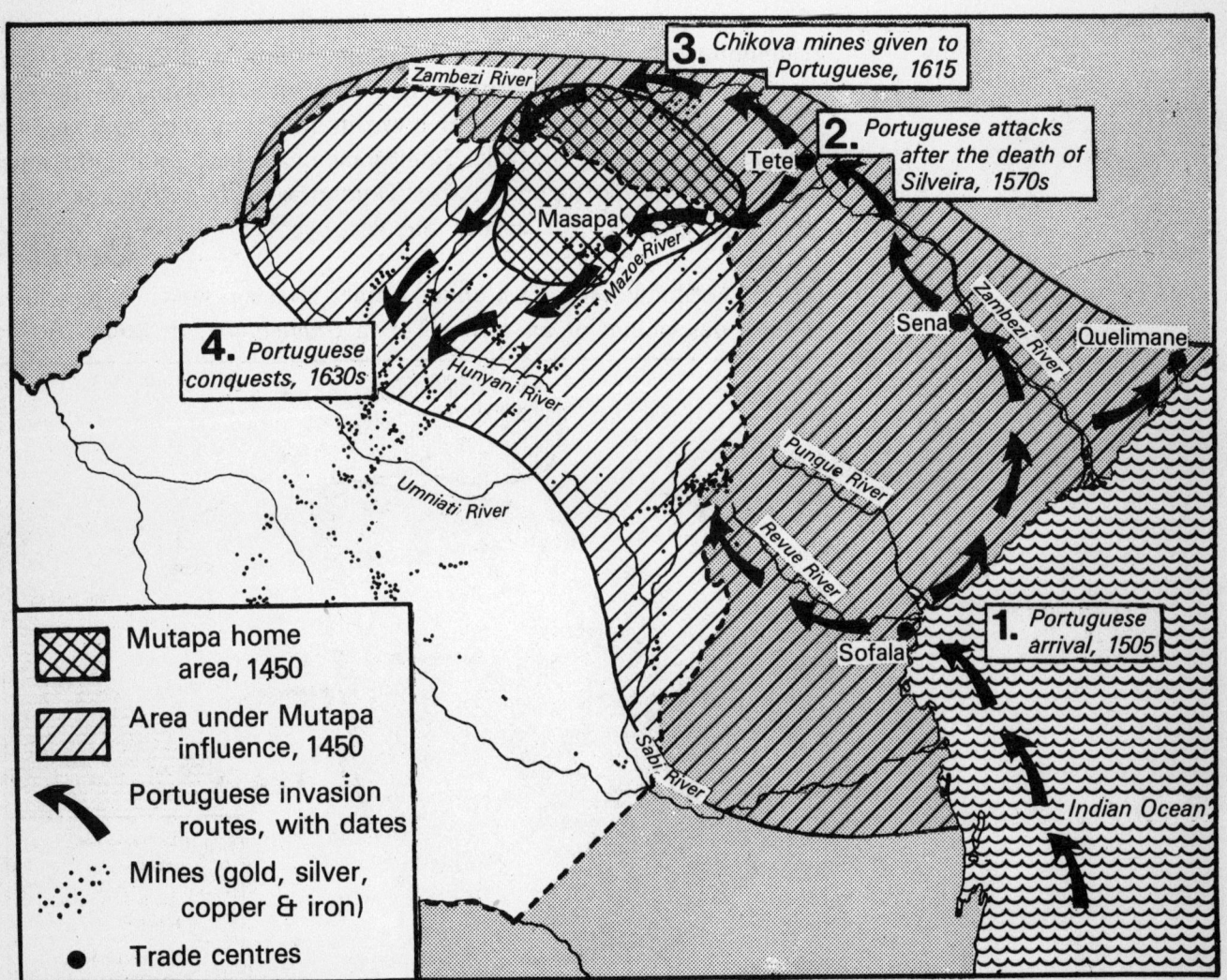

6 The Rozvi Empire

The Portuguese landowners, or *prazeros,* had become very strong by the middle of the 17th century. But they wanted more land and more power. So they went further inland to a country they called Butua, or Guruuswa. They began to build settlements there. But they were stopped by a strong new African leader, the *Changamire* Dombo. He defeated the Portuguese in several battles between 1684 and 1695. He created a powerful state that ruled the plateau for almost 150 years.

Torwa

The Portuguese first wrote about the *Changamire* Dombo in 1684. Before that, they wrote that Butua was ruled by people they called Torwa (or Togwa, Toroa, Toloa). The Torwa had ruled Butua for more than 200 years before Dombo, and sometimes fought against the Munhumutapa. They, too, may have come from Great Zimbabwe. The last time the Portuguese wrote of the Torwa rulers of Butua was in 1683. These writings say there was a civil war in the Torwa state, and the Portuguese were helping one side. Dombo may have been leading the other side against the Portuguese. Afrter Dombo won, the Portuguese called his people Rozvi, which means "the destroyers".

Dombo

We do not know very much about Dombo's background. He may have been a descendant of an earlier Torwa *Changamire,* or leader. Or he

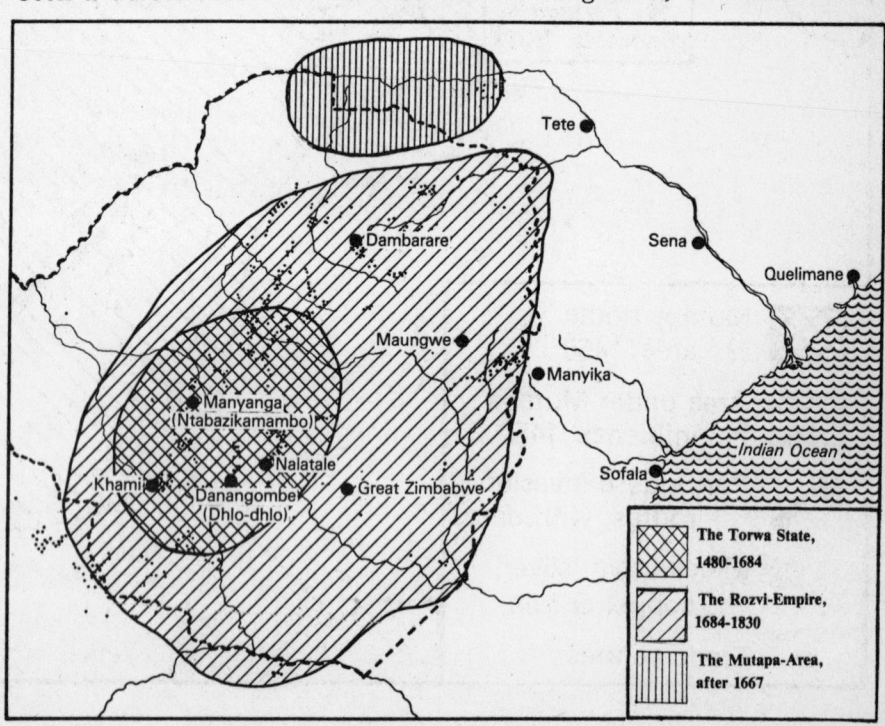

The Torwa State and the Rozvi Empire

could have come from a family with special religious or military duties. Or he could have become rich and powerful through keeping cattle. Perhaps he was all of these things. He may have had links with the Mutapa empire. Some Portuguese **records** say he was once a cowherd of the Munhumutapa. He died in Manyika in 1695, after defeating the Portuguese and sending them out of his country.

After 1695, the Rozvi empire spread to the sandy country of the west and north-west, and to the lowlands of the Limpopo valley. The chiefs of those areas paid tribute to the ruling *Changamire*. His empire covered the whole of Butua and Manyika.

Khami-Type Ruins

The Torwa capital is believed to have been at Khami, near the present city of Bulawayo. The later Rozvi capital may have been in different places at different times — Khami, Danamombe (Dhlodhlo), and Manyanga (Ntabazikamambo). The stone ruins in the Khami area are related to those at Great Zimbabwe. But in some ways they are different. This suggests **evolutionary** change among related people rather than any rapid change caused by outsiders.

The Zimbabwe-type ruins are noted for the free standing walls. These were built in the 13th and 14th century. The Khami-type ruins have platforms, or different levels. Most are dated to the 17th and 18th century, although Khami itself was built earlier. The *Changamire,* or *mambo,* lived in a special house at the highest level. The people and their cattle lived in and around the stone walls lower down.

Way of Life

The Portuguese wrote about a "flat and beautiful plain" bearing rice, pumpkins, watermelons, beans and all sorts of garden greens. The cattle were big and beautiful, like large oxen. They were used as pack animals, as well as for riding. Ostriches were plentiful. Their eggs and feathers were sold at Manyika. There were few trees, so dried cow dung was used in place of firewood. This early Portuguese writing fits the grazing lands between the present cities of Gweru and Bulawayo.

Gold objects found at Danamombe and other sites show the wealth of the Rozvi society. Among these are gold thread for making cloth. The stone ruins show a strong and organized **economy**. External trade prospered, but it was controlled by the state. The Rozvi leaders understood the weaknesses of the Portuguese, and their divisions. So they chose **policies** that made the Portuguese depend on them, and not the other way around. For the next 200 years, the Portuguese tried without success to move into the area. They wanted the regions of great mineral wealth,

Khami, near Bulawayo, showing th platforms of this type of ruins.

Ostrich. The eggs and feathers of this bird were sold in the markets at Manyika.

some of which contain the richest mines to this day. The goldfields of Rimuka. The copper mines at Duma. The iron from Wedza.

Government

The Rozvi *Mambo* ruled with the help of **councillors** who dealt with military and religious affairs, tribute and **administration** of the provinces. Some of the *mambo's* wives played a role at the court. Some of the sons-in-law also had special duties.

The administration was the same as present Shona society, beginning with the hut (*imba*). Then comes the family head (*saimba*), the neighbourhood (*mana*), and its head (*samana*), the village (*musha*) and its head (*samusha*), the region (*dunhu*), sub-chief (*sadunhu*), chiefdom (*nyika*), and the chief (*ishe*). At the top was the *mambo* and his court.

Some important chiefs, such as Manyika (Chikanga) and Mahungwe (Makoni), were likely approved in office by the *mambo*. They were not forced to pay tribute, but they may have chosen to pay tribute in exchange for something else. This tribute would be paid with whatever their region produced, such as cloth, beads, hoes, axes, gold, ivory, cattle, skins, tobacco or food.

Religion

The people of Rozvi believed in one god, Mwari. High priests of Mwari served at a shrine. The priests carried the message from Mwari that people should obey their ancestors. These priests had agents, called *vanyai*, who spread Mwari's word to the regions. They also brought back information. The priests were very powerful. Even the *mambo* had to listen to their advice. The priests remained powerful even after the empire ended and they were among the leaders of the uprising in 1896.

These huts for storing grain have been used by Shona-speaking people for many centuries.

Magical Powers

Oral traditions make many claims about the powers of the Rozvi *mambo*. Some say the *mambo* carried a jug of oil which could kill, or a horn with powerful magic. Some say he could make bees fight for him. Or that he could make rain, or make soldiers brave. Others say he had medicine to send the enemy to sleep or to change the colour of cattle. Some Portuguese records call Dombo a wizard, or magician. This may come from his clever tricks in battle. Or it may come from the story that he ground the bones of his Portuguese enemies after a battle at Dambarare. The story says he used the powder to make his soldiers brave.

Military

Dombo used a new battle plan. Tshaka used the same plan more than 100 years later. The main body of men had two "horns" of soldiers around it. These "horns" could circle around the enemy. When one Rozvi unit was in battle, another unit would stay at the rear. They would treat the wounded and carry supplies. Their most common weapons were bows and arrows. But they also used battle axes, daggers, *assegais*, and spears. They used thick sticks, or clubs, called cudgels. They used shields made from cow hide. The *mambo* often received guns as tribute, and it seems likely that by the 19th century most high-ranking Rozvi officials had guns and knew how to use them.

In spite of this, their weakness seems to have been their belief in peace and their lack of defences. After the defeat of the Portuguese, most of the country lived in peace for more than 100 years. They lived, had children, planted crops, and were at peace with the land. They did not fear enemies. So when the Nguni arrived in the 1830s, the Rozvi were not prepared to fight. The Nguni invasion, and later settler rule, could not dim the oral traditions of the Rozvi as a great and powerful people.

These boys are riding on oxen just as they might have done during the Rozvi period.

VOCABULARY

records	—	written stories of what happened.
evolutionary	—	changing slowly.
economy	—	management and use of goods and money.
policies	—	ways of doing things.
councillors	—	people who give advice, advisers.
administration	—	the way the government works.

Exercises

Summary

The _____ had become very strong by the middle of the _____ century. They tried to go further inland but they were defeated by the _____ _____ in several battles between _____ and _____. The Portuguese called his people _____, which means "the destroyers".

The Rozvi leader ruled with the help of _____. They dealt with _____ and _____ affairs, tribute and administration. The administration was the same as the present _____ society. This begins with the hut (_____). Then the _____ _____ (_____), then _____ (_____) and so on. At the top was the _____ and his court.

Questions

1. Who were the Rozvi and where did they come from?
2. Who was Dombo and how did he become powerful?
3. What is the difference between Zimbabwe-type stone ruins and Khami-type stone ruins?
4. What was the weakness in Rozvi military strategy?

Discuss

The Portuguese *prazeros* wanted to take the mineral resources but the Rozvi would not let them. What are the lessons in this for us today? Why is it still important for us to control our own mineral resources and other natural wealth?

Project

Act out a play about the *mambo* and his court. Choose one person to be the *mambo*. Choose four councillors—for religion, military, tribute and administration. Choose some wives and sons-in-law. Choose some high priests and their agents, the *vanyai*. Then make up a play about something that might have happened. For example, the high priest may receive a message from one of his agents. Then he must go to the councillor for religion, who may take the message to the *mambo* if it is very important. If the message is about defence, then the military adviser would be told, and maybe the sons-in-law. They may call in some soldiers to work out a military plan. They may send the high priest to seek advice from Mwari. The councillor for administration may send people to the provinces to find out what is happening. Or a chief may come to the court from one of the provinces to pay tribute. Choose your own story to act out. From this you can see something of the way a government works. You may want to make up another play about government, set in the present time. For example, a teacher may go to the Ministry of Education and Culture. The teacher may have a problem to tell to an official there. Perhaps there is not enough money, or books or classrooms. That official may take the problem to another official who will take it to the Minister. If it is a very big problem, the Minister may go to the Prime Minister. They may discuss the problem at a meeting of all of the ministers. Or the play could be about the Ministry of Health, or Labour, or Defence. Make up your own story.

Khami-type ruins at Nalatale.

7 Nguni Invaders from the South

Far to the south of the Rozvi, in what is now the Natal province of South Africa, there lived people who spoke Nguni. They worked in their fields, and they kept cattle. Their **political** units were clans, rather than larger groupings.

Tshaka, Zulu Leader

Then came a time of great change. In the early 1800s, many northern Nguni clans were joined together into larger units with more military power. Wars were fought by chiefs to bring about these larger units. This may have occurred because there were more people and cattle and no longer enough land. Among the stronger chiefs were Zwide of the Ndwandwe, Matshobane of the Khumalo, and Dingiswayo of the Mthethwa clans. They had new ways of fighting. They trained the traditional boys' age-sets into highly **disciplined** military units.

Zwide emerged as the strongest chief in the northern Nguni area. But to the south was an even stronger leader. This was Tshaka, of the small Zulu clan. He also had new ideas about warfare. His soldiers used short stabbing spears called *assegais* for hand-to-hand fighting, instead of longer throwing spears. He trained his **regiments** to surround the enemy. His commanders, or *indunas,* reported to him personally for their orders. Using these methods, Tshaka made his Zulu clan into the most powerful state in Southern Africa at that time.

Time of Crushing

Tshaka continued to expand his empire. Nearby groups joined or were defeated. Some fled inland where the Sotho-speaking people lived. They used Tshaka's fighting methods to defeat the Sotho, who were distant relatives. Some Sotho fled west and attacked other groups. Neighbour turned upon neighbour. These movements started a period of war that upset Southern Africa for 15 years, from about 1819 until 1834. The Sotho remember this time as *difaqane,* the "time of crushing". The Nguni call it *mfecane.*

Some Nguni-speaking people moved north across the Limpopo River. One group was led by a man called Soshangane. They took over a large area of what is now south-eastern Zimbabwe and the Gaza province of Mozambique. They are now called the Shangaan.

Another group was led by Zwangendaba. They took many Swazi and Tonga captives, and stayed with Soshangane for a time. Then they moved north-west. They attacked the Rozvi and looted their centres at Khami and Danamombe. In 1834, they reached Manyanga.

Tshaka's Fighting Method

Soldiers formed "horns" around the enemy

They used short stabbing spears

They did not wear shoes

Many years later, an old man called Citsha, who had been a member of Zwangendaba's *impi*, recorded his memories: "Of all the countries we passed through," the old man recalled, "there was one which struck us as the most desirable. This was the country in which a people called the Abalozwi lived. They built their villages in granite hills which they fortified with stone walls. Their chief, *Mambo*, put up a stubborn fight and then fled into the very hilly granite country."

Later, the Mambo and his people were surrounded, the old man said. "They threw down beads and skins and hoes and offered us cattle and sheep to go away and leave them in peace." Then, "they directed us to stand below a certain strange overhanging rock ... it is here that *Mambo* threw himself down in our midst to fall dead and mangled at our feet ... the next day we found that these people had deserted that part of the country during the night and ... we packed up and ... named the hills the Ntabazikamambo."

This left the Rozvi state without a head, but in the villages life went on as before. Zwangendaba continued north across the Zambezi River. His followers spread out into Zambia, Malawi and Tanzania. They are now called the Ngoni.

Zulu soldiers ready for war. See their bare feet, short spears and large shields.

Mzilikazi

Mzilikazi, son of Matshobane of the Khumalo, was born in about 1795. His mother was the daughter of Zwide. Mzilikazi grew up in Zwide's court. Young **heirs** of chiefs were often protected from enemies by living among their mother's people. Mzilikazi grew up during the *mfecane*. He saw how his grandfather dealt with the problem of governing people who were not related. This was a problem that Mzilikazi would later face himself.

Mzilikazi became chief of the Khumalo clan, which was under Zwide's rule. But he later joined Tshaka, perhaps because Zwide had killed his father. After taking many cattle during a raid on the Sotho, Mzilikazi refused to give them to Tshaka. So Tshaka sent a regiment to fight the Khumalo. Many people were killed, but Mzilikazi escaped. He regrouped his people and led them north. After much moving around, they settled north of the Vaal River, in what is now the Transvaal province of South Africa.

People of Mzilikazi

Other Nguni-speaking refugees from Zululand joined them. So did the captured Sotho-Tswana-speaking people. Between 1822 and 1829, the population grew from about 300 to 6 000 people. It was here that Mzilikazi first used the lessons of his grandfather. He brought together people of different origins and cultures into a single nation.

In those early years, Mzilikazi's people called themselves Khumalo, or Zulu, or simply "Mzilikazi's people". The Sotho called them *Matabele*. They gave this name to all Nguni-speaking people from the coast. It meant "men of the long shields" or "those who hide behind their shields". After some time, Mzilikazi's people took the name themselves. They used the Nguni form, *Amandebele*. Today, the English usage shortens this to Ndebele.

Traders and Missionaries

European traders from the Cape coast far to the south went to trade ivory with Mzilikazi. He wanted to learn more about these new arrivals. So he asked the traders to send missionaries to meet him. He knew that these people from the churches were the only Europeans who lived in African areas. This was how he met Robert Moffat of the London Missionary Society. Moffat was his friend for the next 30 years. It was through Moffat that he made contact with the Cape Government. Then Mzilikazi sent a senior adviser, Mncumbatha, to sign an agreement of friendship with them.

Voortrekkers

In 1836, Mzilikazi's state was under attack by the new Zulu leader, Dingane, when it faced another threat — from the Afrikaners. These were Europeans of Dutch descent, sometimes called *Boers*, or farmers. They were not happy with the decision of the British living in the Cape to outlaw **slavery**. They wanted to use cheap African labour. So thousands of Afrikaners left the Cape and moved inland. This was called the "Great Trek". The people were called *Voortrekkers*. They were tough and well led. They had horses and guns, and made good use of them. They moved inland when the people there were weakened by the mfecane. So they easily **occupied** some of the land. When they crossed the Vaal River, they were attacked by Mzilikazi's soldiers. But after several battles, Mzilikazi decided to move north. The *Boers* soon occupied the whole of the Transvaal.

Mzilikazi led his people west to the Tswapong Hills in what is now Botswana. They spent one rainy season there, to rest and plant crops. Then they moved on in smaller groups. Mzilikazi sent one group with his commander Kaliphi (Gundwane) to travel north-east toward the plateau where the Rozvi lived. Mzilikazi continued north toward the Zambezi River.

The Movement of Nguni-speaking People during the *Mfecane*

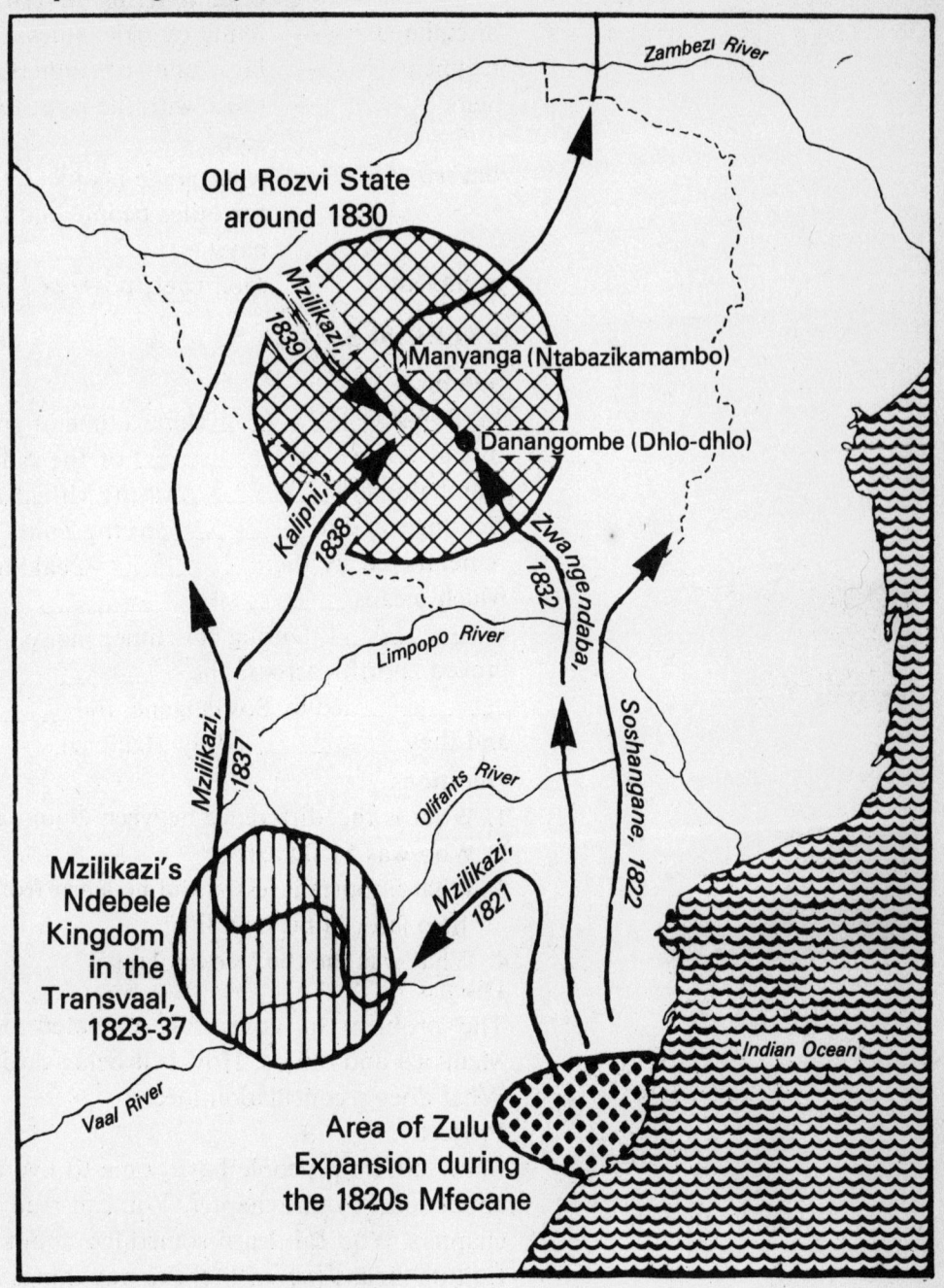

VOCABULARY

political	—	having to do with the way a society is organized and governed.
disciplined	—	living by strict rules, code of conduct.
regiments	—	large units of soldiers.
heirs	—	those with the right to take over as leaders, often sons.
slavery	—	when some people are forced to work very hard for other people and have little or no freedom or pay.
occupied	—	took over, possessed by outside force.

EXERCISES

Summary

In the early _____ came a time of great change. Wars were fought by chiefs such as _____ of the Ndwandwe, _____ of the Khumalo, and _____ of the Mthethwa. They had new ideas about fighting. So did _____ of the Zulu. This time of great change was remembered by the _____ -speaking people as the _____, which means _____ _____ _____. The Nguni called it _____. During this time, many _____ -speaking groups moved north across the _____ River. These included the _____ led by Soshangane, the _____ led by Zwangendaba, and the _____ led by Mzilikazi.

Questions

1. What is the difference between Nguni and Ngoni?
2. Who was Mzilikazi?
3. What important lesson did he learn from his grandfather that was to help later in his own life?
4. What was the the "Great Trek"?

Discuss

The problem of governing unrelated people was faced by Zwide, Mzilikazi and others. How is it being dealt with in Zimbabwe today? What does reconciliation mean?

Project

Many different people have come to live in Zimbabwe. You have read about some in this chapter. You can read about others in the following chapters. You can learn something about other cultures in Zimbabwe. Culture means way of life, the way things are done. This includes traditions, songs, dances, food and drink, ceremonies, stories, and so on. Divide the class into pairs. Each pair of students should ask each other all about their culture, how they do things. Then each student should write a short paper about what they have learned.

8 Arrival of the Ndebele

In 1839, Mzilikazi and some of his people reached the Zambezi River. The rest, led by Kaliphi and others, gathered further south near the Matopos Hills. When Mzilikazi did not join them, there was a **dispute** over who should be king. Some people made his son, Nkulumane, the king. But others who were loyal to Mzilikazi sent scouts north to find him. Mzilikazi rushed back. He defeated the **dissidents** and executed many of them. The fate of Nkulumane was kept secret. Some people said that he was also executed. Others said he was sent away to safety. Mzilikazi joined forces with other Nguni-speaking soldiers in the area. He married a brave woman commander named Nyamazana, and added her Ngoni soldiers to his army.

The Ndebele Nation

Mzilikazi's takeover of what was later called Matabeleland was much more peaceful than his defeat of the Sotho in the Transvaal. There were at least three reasons for this. One reason was that many of the Sotho-Tswana people had deserted the army during the move north. Mzilikazi had fewer soldiers, so he needed to gain power peacefully. Secondly, there was the danger of being chased by the Boers. Mzilikazi wanted to have the local population on his side if that happened. A third reason was the weakness caused by disunity among his own people at that time.

The Shona whom he found living in the area were unified by language and culture. They had a tradition of political unity. But by this time they were living in small **communities** and had few defences. Many of the Shona-speaking chiefs fled into the hills. But they returned to their villages when Mzilikazi promised peace in exchange for their loyalty, grain and young men for his regiments. Cattle raids were carried out against areas further away, to the east and the north, or against chiefs who would not pay tribute. Tribute was usually taken in iron, tools, weapons, jewellery, leather, cattle, grain or services.

Way of Life

The Ndebele grew many crops and kept large herds of cattle. These were an important part of their social life. But sometimes there was not enough rain. Then they had to walk a long way to trade sheep, goats, cattle and beads for grain.

Their society was made up of three **classes.** The *Zansi,* as they were called in the Ndebele language, formed the **aristocracy** or upper class.

Mzilikazi, son of Matshobane of the Khumalo.

41

These were people who had come with Mzilikazi from Zululand, and their relatives. Most of the chiefs were *Zansi*. The next class was the *Nhla*. These were the Sotho-Tswana-speaking people who had been taken into the Ndebele nation. Many of them were soldiers. The lower class were called *Hole*. These were the Shona-speaking people. The *Zansi* were the smallest group. The *Hole* were the largest. They spread their culture and beliefs to the other two.

Mzilikazi ruled with the advice of two councils. The *mphakati* was made up of some of his relatives, and a few chosen chiefs. They made the final decisions on national issues after these had been discussed by a larger assembly, called *izikhulu*. This included chiefs and elders noted for their **wisdom** and knowledge of traditional customs.

Religion

All three classes believed in the wisdom of their ancestors, who spoke through spirit mediums. For *Zansi,* the ancestors of the king were most important. The king, through his priests, prayed to them for rain and good crops. The *Zansi* also believed in a high god called Nkulunkulu, but he played no part in their daily life.

During the time in the Transvaal, the Ndebele had begun to take the *Molimo* beliefs of the Tswana. When they came further north they adopted the Shona god, Mwari, but continued to call him by the Tswana name, *Molimo*. The Ndebele kings sent gifts to the priests at the shrines of Mwari. They often visited the spirit mediums. During times of drought they prayed to Mwari.

Every year, at the start of the long rains, the *Zansi* held the ceremony of *Inxwala*. Cattle were given as a sacrifice to the king's ancestors, and the nation prayed for good crops and success in battle.

Military

The Ndebele army was made up of many regiments totalling about 20 000 men. Regiments were placed in the towns and each *induna* was chosen by the king. He also appointed four provincial commanders. These commanders and senior *indunas* advised the king on military matters.

Mzilikazi built many chief towns but his real capital was wherever he was. He was always moving about, visiting different parts of the nation. He travelled with many advisers and bodyguards, many wives who prepared his food and beer, and a large herd of cattle. One or more of his wives lived in each town, where they represented him. Except for a few royal *Zansi* wives, these women and their children lived as ordinary people.

Lobengula

Mzilikazi died in 1868. Lobengula became the next ruler of the society his father had created. The society had survived because it could move from place to place. It had grown because Mzilikazi knew how to govern unrelated peoples. But it contained seeds of disunity which burst when Lobengula came to power.

Many people believed that the heir, Nkulumane, was still alive. Two years were spent searching for him, while a council of three trusted advisers ruled the nation. These were Mncumbata Khumalo, a cousin of the king; Budaza, another relative; and Gwabalanda Mate, the *induna enkulu* at the big town, Mhlahlandlela, where Lobengula had grown up. Finally, Mncumbata announced that Nkulumane was dead, that he had been killed by his father. But some people still did not believe this. One of these was Mbiko, leader of the regiment which had turned back an Afrikaner invasion 20 years earlier. Many of the *Zansi* clans thought their chief should rule the nation. Some of the *Nhla* chiefs thought they should rule. Mbiko did not want Lobengula to be king because he was the son of a Swazi woman.

Battle of Zwangendaba

Europeans in the south claimed to have found Nkulumane in Natal. But the council installed Lobengula as king in 1870. Royal doctors gave him medicine and charms. The Mwari priests blessed him. This made him popular among his people, most of whom were Shona-speaking. When it came to the final battle with Mbiko, Lobengula won. This was the battle of Zwangendaba.

Mbiko's men had many guns. But Lobengula had more soldiers, most of them *Hole*. He had tried to avoid the battle, but he was ambushed by Mbiko's men. After Mbiko was killed, Lobengula pardoned the other rebels. He spoke of his deep sadness over the death of so many people.

After this, Lobengula moved his capital to a new place and called it Bulawayo. Lobengula moved people around so that the rebels, who were *Zansi,* were living among the loyal Kalanga and Rozvi of the *Hole* class. A person claiming to be Nkulumane tried several times to invade. He was supported by Europeans in the south who wanted to look for gold. Finally they accepted that Lobengula was king and they would have to talk to him.

Lobengula became the Ndebele king at a big ceremony in 1870. This is an artist's drawing.

Mzilikazi's son, Lobengula.

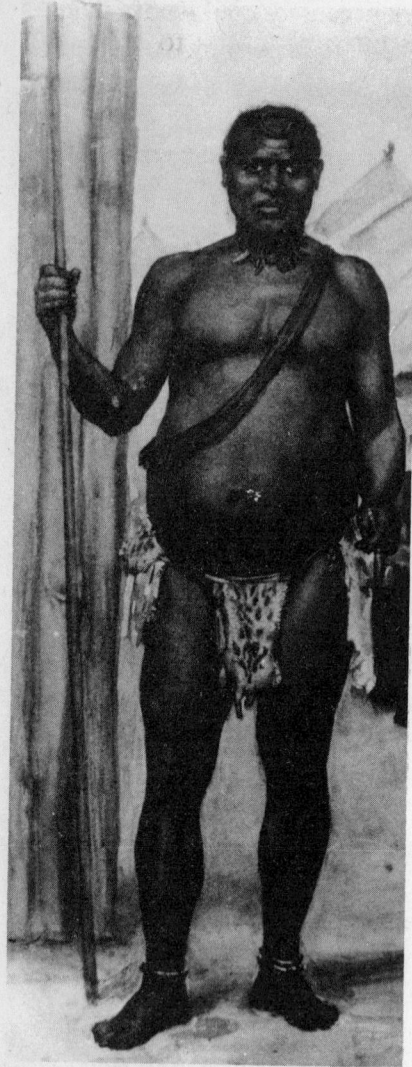

Lobengula once said, "Did you ever see a chameleon catch a fly? The chameleon gets behind the fly and remains motionless for some time. Then he advances very slowly and gently, first putting forward one leg and then another. At last, when well within reach, he darts his tongue and the fly disappears. England is the chameleon and I am that fly."

VOCABULARY

dispute	—	argument, difference.
dissidents	—	people who no longer agree with those in power.
communities	—	places where people live and often share many things in common.
classes	—	groups in a society ranked by birth or wealth or power.
aristocracy	—	the upper class, by title, rank or birth.
wisdom	—	having great knowlwdge, and wise thoughts.

EXERCISES

Summary

Some people tried to make _____ the king. But others brought back Mzilikazi. Many of the _____ -speaking chiefs had fled into the hills. But they came back when he promised them _____ in return for their _____, _____, and young men for his regiments. Ndebele society had three classes. These were the _____, _____, and _____. Mzilikazi ruled them with the advice of two councils, the _____ and the _____. All three classes believed in the wisdom of their _____ spirits. When they came north Mzilikazi's people adopted the Shona god, _____ but called him by the Tswana name, _____.

Questions

1. Why did Mzilikazi want to win the support of the Shona rather than fighting against them?
2. What was the importance of the ancestors in the Ndebele nation?
3. Who advised the king on military matters?
4. Why was there disunity when Lobengula came to power?

Discuss

Compare the classes in the Ndebele society you have just read about to classes in the Zimbabwe society today. What determines class today — is it money, or power, or birth? Is it possible to have a classless society where everyone is equal?

Project

Ask someone from the district council to come and explain to the students how the government works today. Compare that to the governments in the Munhumutapa, Rozvi and Ndebele societies.

9 The Growth of Imperialism

During the 19th century, there were many changes in Europe. These were caused by the **Industrial Revolution**, which began in Britain. This meant that industry grew very quickly. Many things were no longer made by hand. They were made by machines. Cloth and other goods were made much faster. But the workers in Europe were paid very little money. They worked hard but they were poor. They did not have money to buy all of these new goods. So the owners began to look for other places to sell their goods. The owners became very rich. They had a lot of money, or capital. They were **capitalists**, so they wanted more money and power. They began to look outside their own countries for **raw materials** and markets.

These capitalists began to put money into mining in Africa. They began to **exploit** the mineral wealth of Africa. They sent Europeans to live in Africa to run the mines for them. These Europeans sent raw materials to Europe and bought machine-made goods. They did not think about the Africans living in these **colonies**. They exploited their labour and took their land. European governments agreed with this because they wanted to expand their empires. This belief in having colonies and building empires is called imperialism. That means that people in one country are told what to do by the government of another country.

A cartoon of the times from a magazine called Vanity Fair, shows Rhodes and other imperialists planning the takeover of Africa.

"Darkest Africa"

People in Europe did not know very much about Africa. They did not know about African people, or African history, or African life. Few Europeans had been inland in Africa. They were **explorers** and missionaries, like David Livingstone. They often told stories about "darkest Africa". Some said Africans were savages who fought all the time, and often ate other people. So people in Europe got a distorted idea of Africa. The European churches thought Africans had no God. So they sent missionaries to spread their religious beliefs about Christ, called Christianity. Some said they were bringing **civilization**. They did not learn about the civilizations that already existed.

Scramble for Africa

More European countries sent people to Africa. Their governments began to worry about losing out. They feared that other countries would get the trade or the mining, and become more powerful. The Belgians, British, French, Germans and Portuguese all took part in the "Scramble for Africa". People from those countries met in Berlin, Germany, in 1884, to discuss their interest in Africa. They agreed on areas where each country could operate. But they also decided that each country which claimed an area must send people to occupy it, or lose the claim.

So European countries began to colonize the whole of Africa. They said they were bringing peace and ending slavery. But they got rich themselves, and they brought a new form of slavery. They crushed the existing African ways of government, economy and culture. They forced European ways on the people. European governments sent their people to take land, make laws, and force Africans to accept their rule. This was often done by giving rights, called charters, to companies. These were called chartered companies.

Cecil Rhodes

Britain moved quickly to colonize the area north of the Limpopo River. This was done through the British South Africa Company (BSAC). The area was later named "Rhodesia" after the head of the BSAC, Cecil John Rhodes.

Rhodes was born in England in 1853, the son of a minister. He was often sick as a child. So his father sent him to South Africa where he hoped the warm weather would be good for his health. Rhodes made a lot of money from the diamond mines. His company, De Beers, still controls the world's diamond market. Rhodes was an imperialist. He believed in expanding the British Empire. He believed that British people and British companies should take over Africa from the Cape, in the south, to Cairo (Egypt) in the north. First he had to stop the Boers from taking the area north of the Limpopo River.

Cecil Rhodes was an imperialist who believed that Britain should rule Africa.

Lobengula welcomed missionaries and traders but they did not always tell him the truth.

The Boers or the British

Mzilikazi made a treaty, or agreement, with the Boers in 1853. Then Afrikaner hunters and traders could enter Matabeleland. The English-speaking settlers in the Cape Colony began to worry that the Boers would take all of the land. They wanted the Limpopo River to be the northern border of the Afrikaner country.

Then the Boers found gold in the Transvaal. They thought there might be more gold in the north. In 1887, the Boers sent Piet Grobler to visit Lobengula. Grobler signed a treaty that said Lobengula was an "ally" of the Boers. Lobengula may have wanted a peace treaty. He knew the power of the Europeans' guns and he did not want a war with them. But maybe he did not know what else the treaty said. It said he would help the Boers and put his men under Boer command.

The Boers said the Grobler Treaty gave them mining rights in Matabeleland. So the British made plans to occupy the area and stop the Boers from taking it. In 1888, a British missionary named John Moffat arrived in Bulawayo. He was the son of Robert Moffat, who had been friendly with Mzilikazi. The younger Moffat asked Lobengula to deal with the British. He said the Boers were planning to invade Matabeleland.

John Moffat.

Moffat Treaty

Moffat came with another British missionary, Rev. Charles Helm. He had been trying to convert the Ndebele to Christianity. Lobengula, like his father, allowed the missionaries to come and he treated them well. But very few Ndebele accepted the new religion. They kept their Nguni, Sotho, Tswana and Shona customs. The missionaries decided that this religion must be destroyed. But Lobengula trusted Helm. Helm helped Moffat to get an agreement with Lobengula. This was called the Moffat Treaty. Lobengula said the Grobler Treaty was "not my words". Moffat and Helm did not tell Lobengula that Rhodes was giving them a lot of money to get this new treaty.

The treaty said that Lobengula would not sell land, or make other treaties, without asking the British Government. On the back of the treaty, Helm wrote that he had explained what it said. These treaties were written in European languages by Europeans. Mzilikazi and Lobengula could not read. So they had to ask the same people who wrote the treaties to tell them what the treaties said. Many of these people did not tell them everything.

After the Moffat Treaty, the British government said Lobengula was the ruler of Matabeleland and Mashonaland. But he was not the ruler of Mashonaland. This was a British warning to the Portuguese who were trading in Mashonaland.

Rev. C. D. Helm.

47

Rudd Concession

Lobengula's court soon filled with people wanting concessions. That means they wanted rights to mine or trade in his kingdom. Each person promised something in return, such as money or goods. Finally in 1888, Lobengula put his mark on a paper giving mining rights to Charles Rudd. This was called the Rudd Concession. The paper said no one else could look for minerals in his kingdom. Rudd promised to pay $135 a month, plus 1,000 rifles, 100,000 rounds of ammunition, and a gun-boat on the Zambezi River. Or $675 in cash. Rudd sold the concession to Rhodes' company for more than one million dollars.

The Boers sent people to see Lobengula. They told him he had sold his country. Lobengula was very upset. He sent two advisers to Britain to tell the queen that he had been tricked. Rudd had not told him the truth about what the paper said. Rhodes got very angry because he was trying to get a Royal Charter from Queen Victoria for his BSA Company. So he worked out a plan to kill Lobengula and take his land. But one of his men got drunk and talked about the plan. So it had to be dropped.

Lobengula's men had gone to London with E.M. Maund, who said he was against Rhodes. But Maund also tricked Lobengula and sold his company to Rhodes. Queen Victoria told Lobengula's men that her government had agreed to give a charter to the BSAC. Lobengula then made a public statement saying he did not agree to the Rudd Concession. This did not stop Rhodes from wanting Matabeleland. On the basis of the Rudd Concession, the British South Africa Company planned an invasion through Mashonaland.

Charles Rudd.

VOCABULARY

Industrial Revolution	— revolution means very fast changes. These fast changes in industry were caused by the use of new machines.
capitalists	— people who control a lot of money, or capital, and use it to make more money.
raw materials	— materials used in industry to make other things. Iron ore is a raw material for making steel. Cotton is a raw material before it is spun into thread and woven into cloth.
exploit	— to use people or resources to make money for yourself, often without paying the full value.
colonies	— places ruled by people in another country.
explorers	— people who travel into a place to learn about it.
civilization	— a highly developed social system.

EXERCISES

Summary
The Boers claimed that the _____ Treaty of 1887 gave them mining rights in _____. So the _____ made plans to occupy the area and stop the Boers from taking it. In _____, a British missionary named _____ _____ arrived at Bulawayo. He was the son of _____ _____. He met with another missionary called _____ _____. They did not tell Lobengula they were paid a lot of money by _____. After the _____ Treaty, the British said Lobengula was ruler of both _____ and _____. Lobengula gave a mining concession to _____ _____, who sold it to _____. On the basis of the _____ _____, the _____ _____ _____ company prepared its invasion.

Questions
1. What was the "Scramble for Africa"? When was it? And which European countries were involved?
2. Who was Cecil Rhodes?
3. Why did he send Moffat, Rudd and others to meet Lobengula?
4. How did the Industrial Revolution in Europe lead to imperialisim in Africa?

Discuss
Underdevelopment. Most countries in Africa are underdeveloped. They were used by other countries and their wealth was taken away. They were exploited by capitalist companies which used their labour and took the land and raw materials. These companies did not pay the full value. Often they did not pay at all. In this way, African were robbed of the wealth created by their own labour and natural resources. This still happens today in many countries, and they are very poor. How can a country like ours stop underdevelopment?

Project
Study the map in this chapter titled "The Scramble for Africa". Trace the map into your notebook. Draw the European countries and the African colonies as they are on the map. Then, on the map in your notebook, draw a line from each European country to one of its colonies. Look at the key and draw a line from Britain to a colony with the same pattern, for example, Rhodesia (Zimbabwe). Draw a line from Portugal to a colony with the same pattern, for example, Portuguese East

Africa (Mozambique). And so on. These lines will show you something about colonial development and underdevelopment. Transport systems such as railways, and ports for ships, were built to take raw materials from the colony to Europe. Postal services, and later telephones, were set up so the company in Europe would knew about events in the colony. Such things were not built to help business within Africa, or between African countries. They were built in the interests of capitalism, imperialism and colonialism.

The Scramble for Africa

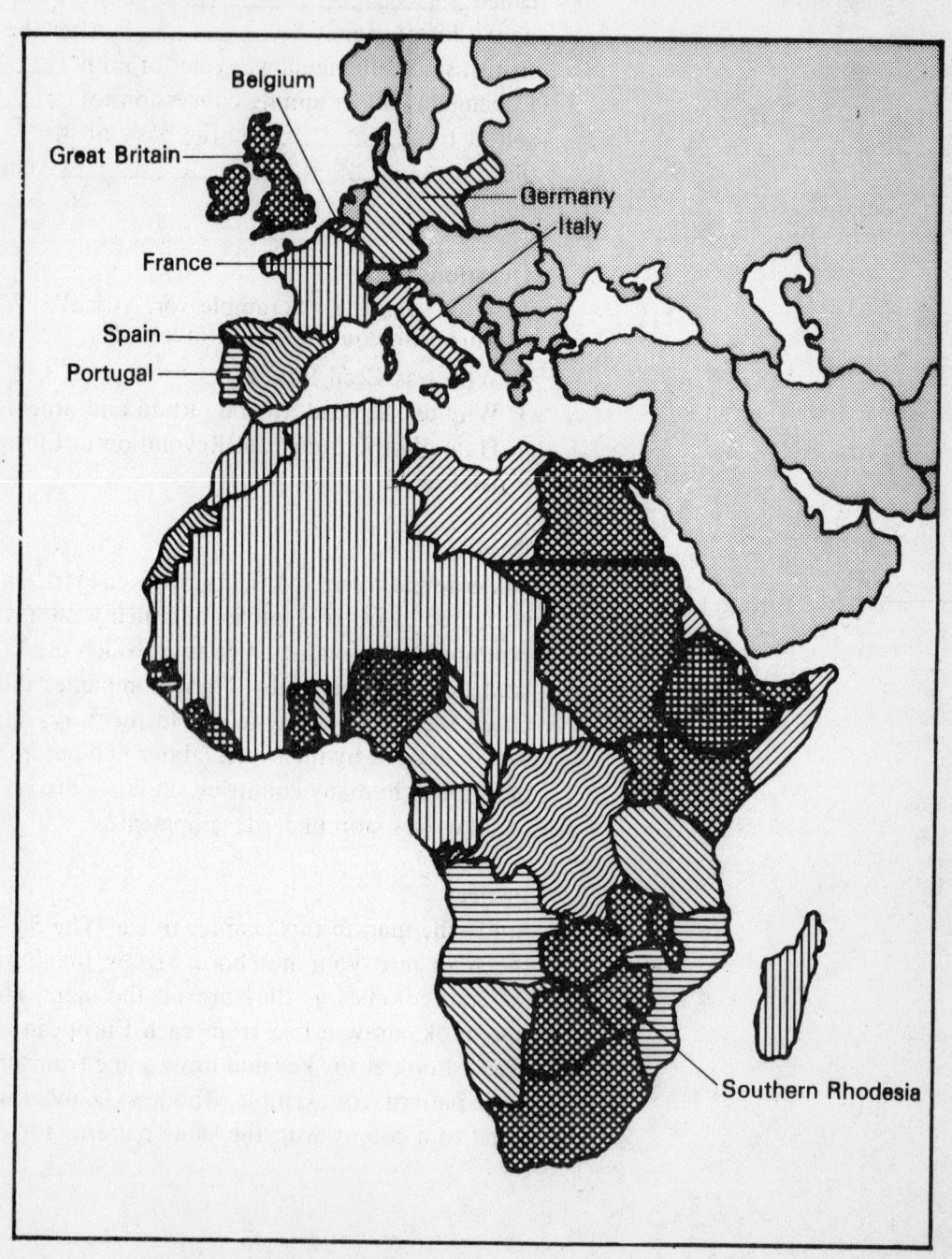

10 European Occupation

Europeans occupied Mashonaland in 1890, and Matabeleland in 1893. Both invasions were organized by the British South Africa Company, and agreed to by the British Government. Both were by **mercenary** forces. They were well armed and each man was offered a large sum of money. Each man was told he could have some mining claims and some land. Most of the men were looking for gold. The BSAC called them **pioneers**. The plateau was occupied and colonial rule was forced upon Africans with little offered in return. The Company stole their land and then forced them to work on it.

European ivory hunters with elephant tusks.

Invasion of Mashonaland

The BSAC chose 200 European men who could ride horses and use guns, in case Lobengula sent soldiers to stop them. They wore military uniforms. They were armed with small guns called revolvers. They had simple machine-guns and big guns mounted on wheels, called artillery. Three hundred European policemen rode with them. Major Frank Johnson organized the invasion. He promised each man 15 claims in the goldfields and 3 000 acres of land. This added up to more than one and a half million acres of Mashonaland.

The men on horseback, with wagons drawn by oxen, crossed the Macloutsie River from Bechuanaland (Botswana) in June 1890. They followed a way chosen by the hunter-explorer Frederick Courtenay Selous. They gave colonial names to places where they rested, such as Fort Victoria and Fort Charter. They stopped when they got to Harare Hill. They raised the British flag on 12 September 1890, and said they were taking the area for the British queen. They set up a town at Harare. They named it Salisbury after the British Prime Minister at that time. For the next 70 years, the Europeans celebrated "Occupation Day". In 1961, it was changed to "Pioneer Day". It is no longer a holiday in Zimbabwe.

They raised the British flag on Harare Hill and claimed the area for the British queen, Victoria.

Racial Prejudice

These Europeans hoped to find gold or other riches in the area they called Mashonaland. When they did not find much gold, some took land and began to farm. More **settlers** came from Europe and South Africa. They knew little about African customs. They often made up stories about African life. In most cases, they did not think of African feelings at all. They brought a new sort of alcohol that was very strong, and diseases such as smallpox and measles. They had the only medicine to

Covered wagon crossing stream.

Many crops were grown by African farmers

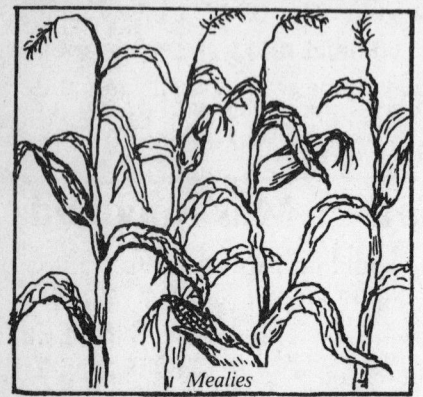

Cabbages

Mealies

Pumpkins

Millet

cure these new diseases. And they brought racial prejudice. That was their belief that Europeans were better than Africans, and had the right to rule. The men who had come before, such as the Portuguese and the Ndebele, often married Shona women and became part of their life. These new settlers did not do that. Some had children by African women, but few married or learned the language and customs. They did not try to see things the African way. They came with their own ideas which they thought were better.

The settlers did not respect the authority of the **paramount** chiefs they found living on the land — Makoni Mutota Chirimaunga of Maungwe, Soswe of Mbire, Mtoko of Budja, Marange of Bocha, Mangwende of Nohwe, Mutasa of Manyika, and others. The settlers ignored the existing African form of government that included courts. They forced upon the people the Company's harsh and unjust rule. The people called it "Charter Ro".

Food and Peace

For the first 20 years most of the settlers' food was grown by African farmers. Some of the first settlers kept notes about what they saw. One wrote of the "rich and fertile country" where "cattle lowed in every valley". Another wrote of the wide range of food grown by African farmers: "Mealies, poko corn, kaffir corn, millet, groundnuts, beans (five sorts), eggs, fruit, cabbages, sweet potatoes, peas, pumpkins of sorts, watermelons, cucumbers, chillies, tobacco, bananas, and lemons".

The Europeans were received peacefully. One old man said later: "We saw you come with your wagons and horses and rifles, and we said to each other 'They come to buy gold, or maybe to hunt elephant. They will go again.' But when we saw that you continued to remain in the country and were troubling us with your laws we began to talk and plot."

Lippert Concession

At first, the British government would not allow the Company to make laws. They said the Rudd Concession gave rights only for mining. So Rhodes gave a lot of money to a German banker called Lippert to get another treaty. Lippert told Lobengula that he was against Rhodes. Lippert said he was thinking of the rights of the Ndebele people. But this was not true. Lobengula believed what Lippert said and gave him a concession over land. Lobengula did not rule over the land in Mashonaland, the Shona chiefs did. But the Company used this concession to take their land.

Who Owns the Land

A Shona chief could not sell the land on which his people lived, and where their ancestors were buried. He could only lend the land to a person to use. The land did not belong to him. It belonged to all of the people. That way of doing things is now called **socialism,** or **communism**. The community owns the land and the natural resources, and these are used for the good of all the people. But the settlers were capitalists. They believed in the power of money. They believed in private ownership of land. Each settler got papers from the Company which said he owned some land.

Lobengula's land

The British South Africa Company found little gold in Mashonaland. So they turned their eyes back to Lobengula's land. The senior Company official in Mashonaland was Leander Starr Jameson. He ordered Captain Allan Wilson to find men for another invasion. Each man was promised 6 000 acres of land in Matabeleland and 20 claims in the goldfields. They were also told they could steal what they could carry away. Half of this would go to the Company and they could keep the rest. Rhodes agreed to the invasion. He lived in the Cape where he was Prime Minister of the Colony.

Invasion of Matabeleland

Jameson tried to hide his plans for an invasion. He wanted to find a way to make the Ndebele attack first. So he sent his soldiers to chase away a Ndebele regiment near **Masvingo.** The regiment had gone to raid a chief who did not pay his tribute to Lobengula. They were under orders not to fight against the Europeans. Many were captured and killed by Jameson's men.

Lobengula still wanted peace. He sent a letter to the British queen. But his messengers were killed before they moved very far. He sent another messenger to take money to the invaders, to ask them to go away and leave him in peace. Two European soldiers kept the money and did not pass on the message. Lobengula had hoped to keep his country free through talking rather than fighting. But he learned that it was not possible to talk to people who could not be trusted.

War was forced on Lobengula in October 1893. His country was invaded by a force of more than 1 000 Europeans with 2 000 soldiers and police from Bechuanaland. His soldiers fought bravely, but they were not prepared and many were ill with smallpox. Their light guns and rifles were not match for the invaders' machine-guns and artillery. The in-

Lobengula's envoys.

vaders took no prisoners. They killed all wounded Ndebele soldiers. When they reached Bulawayo, they found that Lobengula had burnt his village and left. He had given orders that Europeans living in Bulawayo were not to be hurt.

Lobengula and a few advisers moved north-west down the Shangani River. A small European force led by Captain Wilson tried to follow Lobengula but they were defeated in battle. Lobengula died soon after, in January 1894. His burial place was kept secret.

Jameson remained in Bulawayo to distribute the stolen goods, called loot, and the land. More than 90 000 cattle were taken. Lobengula's people were forced off the best land into reserves. They were not allowed to plant food until they had given up their weapons, so many of them starved. This was made worse by drought, locusts, and a cattle disease called rinderpest. Thousands of healthy cattle were shot by the settlers to stop the spread of the disease. Africans in Matabeleland owned at least 200 000 cattle in 1893. Four years later, there were less than 14 000 cattle owned by Africans in the whole country.

After peace was restored, Rhodes went to Bulawayo. He built his house at the place where Lobengula's house had been. Next to Lobengula's Indaba Tree, he built another house, for future governors. Lobengula's kingdom became part of "Rhodesia".

Ndebele Terrritory and The Pioneer Route, 1890

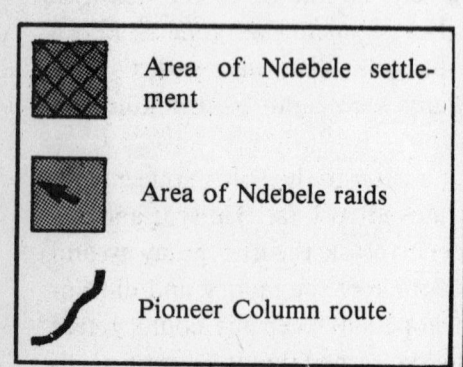

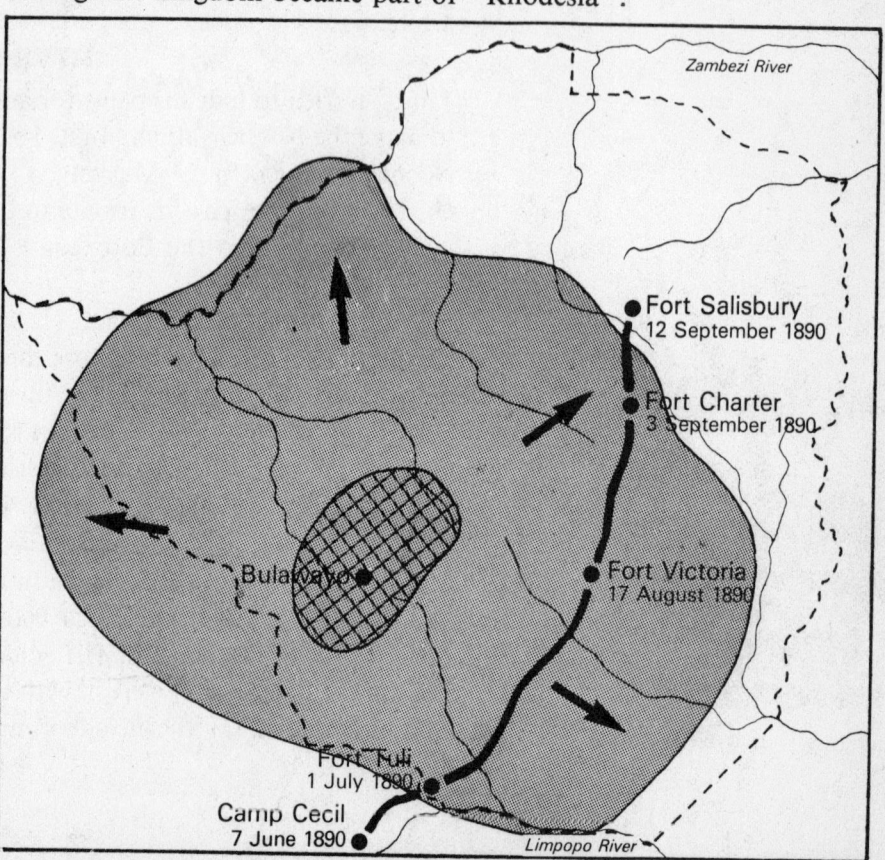

VOCABULARY

mercenary	—	person who takes up arms to fight outside his own country because he is promised money.
pioneers	—	the first members of a group to arrive in a place.
settlers	—	people who come from somewhere else to live in a place.
paramount	—	most important, senior.
socialism	—	a system in which the land, natural resources, and main industries are owned by the people and managed by their government.
communism	—	scientific socialism, in which property is owned by the community and used for the good of all of its members.

EXERCISES
Summary
The _____ government said the Rudd Concession gave rights only for _____. The _____ Concession gave rights for land. But the land in _____ did not belong to _____. The BSAC found little _____ in _____. So they decided to invade _____. The invasion was organized by _____, the senior Company official in _____. It was approved by _____. War was forced on _____ in October _____. The invaders killed all wounded _____ soldiers. But _____ gave orders that _____ living in _____ were not to be harmed.

Questions
1. Describe the force that occupied Mashonaland in 1890.
2. Who were some of the paramount chiefs they found living on the land?
3. Why did Lobengula try to avoid war? Why did he fail?

Discuss
The land. Who owns the land under socialism? Who owns the land under capitalism? Whom do you think should own the land, and why?

Project
In this chapter you read about the crops grown by African farmers on the plateau about 100 years ago. Go to your school garden and check which of these crops are grown there. Learn to identify them from their leaves. Then plant some of the other crops on the list that are not in your school garden. Remember to pull the weeds and water the plants. Watch them grow, and learn about the ones you have not seen before.

11 The First Chimurenga

Africans on the plateau soon learned the meaning of "Charter Ro". It meant their way of life was changed completely. Most of their land and many of their cattle were taken. They were forced to work for the settlers. The power of the chiefs was reduced. If they did something the settlers did not like, their huts and crops were burnt. Often they were beaten. Sometimes they were shot.

Oppression

The BSA Company said the Lippert Concession allowed them to give the land to the settlers. But the paramount chiefs did not like this. They were stopped from trading with the Portuguese. Their land was given away to strangers until there were European farms all round them. Their people could not plant crops freely or graze their cattle and goats. They often had to pay rent to use their own land. Company officials made their own laws. An African could be shot for theft or for hitting a European. When one man hit a settler who accused him of theft, 23 members of his family were shot. The kraal and crops of a chief were burnt because some of his men were found wearing boots. This harsh and unjust treatment of people is called oppression.

Hut Tax

The oppression got worse with the Hut Tax in 1893. Any settler could collect from Africans in his area a tax of ten shillings for each hut. Most Africans had no means of making money to pay the tax. So their cattle, goats or sheep were taken. The men were forced to work on roads, or buildings, or European farms. Sometimes the men were forced to work for one month then treated badly so they would leave without their pay. When a chief sent too few workers, the police went to his village to collect more.

The people were getting very angry with the police. So the Company set up a Native Department to deal with Africans and collect Hut Tax. The Department had its own agents, or Native Commissioners, and did not use the police. But the chiefs were still angry about the Hut Tax. They did not see why the invaders should make laws, or take tribute or tax. There had been no agreements, and they had not been defeated. Yet their life had changed so much that people rushed into the hills with their cattle when they saw the Native Commissioner coming. The Hut Tax was the last of many **grievances** that caused the war of 1896 that is now called the First Chimurenga.

"Charter Ro"

The oppression in Matabeleland was even harsher. After the 1893 war, almost all land and most Ndebele cattle were taken. Cattle raiding by

Collecting the Hut Tax. This tax forced Africans to work for the settlers.

Company agents went on until late 1895. The land was given freely by the Company as payment to the invaders, and to new companies formed by other British capitalists. Lobengula's people were given poorer land, in places later called "Native Reserves". Most refused to go. They stayed on European farms where they had to pay rent. Or they moved about from place to place. They also had to pay the Hut Tax, and were forced to work for the settlers.

The Ndebele leaders were angry about the harsh BSAC rule. They were angry about losing their land and their cattle. They were afraid their people would go without food. So they began to unite to fight their **oppressors**.

Early settler house, Imbedza.

Jameson Raid

The events of late December 1895 gave them the chance they were waiting for. Dr. Jameson, the Company administrator, took most of the police on a raid into the Transvaal. He was trying to overthrow the Boer President, Paul Kruger. Rhodes, who was Prime Minister of the Cape, agreed to the raid. He wanted the rich gold mines in the Transvaal. He wanted to add the whole of southern Africa to the British empire. But the Jameson Raid failed. Jameson and 400 members of his force were arrested by the Boers. Rhodes had to resign as Cape Prime Minister. A few months later, he was forced to resign as a director of the British South Africa Company. But more important for events in Rhodesia, Jameson had left only 48 European mounted police in the whole country.

Uprising in Matebeleland

Many Ndebele *indunas* were working on European farms. They had been dealing with European agents for years, and knew them well. They had urged Lobengula to fight the Europeans. They were angry about the long history of dishonest dealings. They were angry about the 1893 invasion. When the time came to fight again, they were organized by Umlugulu, the Ndebele high priest, Lobengula's son Nyamanda, and a young *induna* called Mpotshwana. These Ndebele leaders joined the Rozvi priests of Mwari to organize the people for war. The priests came from four shrines. These shrines were centres of information, education, and religious teaching. So it was easy for the priests to move among the people telling them that Mwari wanted them to send away the Europeans. The most important priest was Mkwati, from the shrine at Ntabazikamambo. He was married to the daughter of a Rovzi chief. He often travelled into Mashonaland with his assistants, Siginyamatshe, and a woman called Tenkela. They preached unity against a common enemy. Their religious beliefs helped to overcome old divisions among the people.

An African police unit was ambushed on 20 March 1896. Four days later the first European was killed. Within a week, 130 settlers living on farms or in mining camps in Matabeleland had been killed. The rest fled to the towns. The Ndebele soldiers had a lot of ammunition. They were better at shooting than they had been in 1893. They knew the land and knew where to retreat. Africans who worked in the BSAC police deserted. They took with them their guns and their knowledge of the BSAC. Suddenly, the white settlers who had been sure of their own power found themselves in great danger and were afraid.

Indaba with Rhodes

The British government sent Imperial forces to defend the settlers. The Company had to pay the cost of the Imperial forces. When it began to cost too much money, Rhodes sent a message to Umlugulu asking to talk. The younger Ndebele soldiers did not want to talk to Rhodes. But Umlugulu and others insisted. Fields and homes all over Matabeleland had been burnt by white patrols, and there was little food left. More fighting would mean no time to plant, and many people would starve. So Umgululu and about 40 *indunas* met Rhodes and his officers in the Matopos Hills on 21 August 1896.

In a series of meetings, or *indabas*, over the next two months, the chiefs told Rhodes why they were angry with the BSAC and the settlers. Rhodes promised to change some things. He told the Ndebele leaders that their powers would be returned. He agreed to pay salaries to the chiefs. The people who had fought in Matabeleland were **pardoned**. Many of the settlers were angry at Rhodes for making this agreement.

Revolt in Mashonaland

There had been unrest in some parts of Mashonaland. Chief Kunzwi-Nyandoro would not allow Native Police to collect hut tax in his area. He sent a message that all police and white men who entered would be killed. Other chiefs did the same. But the settlers were not worried. They did not think the Shona chiefs would fight. So they were not prepared. Most European men were fighting in Matabeleland.

The **revolt** in Western Mashonaland began on 18 June 1896, in Mashayamombe's area near Chegutu. It spread rapidly. Fires were lit on tops of hills from district to district to spread the news. Some of Mangwende's people, led by his son Muchemwa, attacked a store near Marondera. They joined forces with some of Makoni's people led by his son Mhiripiri, to attack a police post nearby. And so on. Soon the Harare to Mutare road was cut off. By the end of June, there was not a European left between Harare and the Zambezi valley.

Prisoners chained together, Bulawayo.

Nehanda and Kaguvi

Many paramount chiefs led their people in raids on settler farms. They ambushed Company patrols. They knew where to hide and when to retreat. They were acting on the advice of the most powerful members of their community, the spirit mediums. The Chegutu area, where the uprising began, had been the home of the medium of Chaminuka. He organized the **resistance** to the Nguni invaders many years earlier. His kraal at Chitungwiza is still a sacred place. In the same area, in 1896, came the medium of Kaguvi. He was Gomboreshumba, the "lion's paw". He was a good organizer and he was well known. He had worked in Chiquaqua's area. He was the son-in-law of Mashonganyika. He was consulted by Nyandoro.

Kaguvi was joined by another medium from the Mazoe valley whom the settlers feared as "the most important wizard in Mashonaland". She was the medium of Nehanda. Nehanda was the daughter of Mutota and sister to the first Munhumutapa, Matope. Nehanda and Kaguvi, with Wamponga, Gorongo, and others, joined the priests of Mwari in giving unity and direction to the revolt. With their knowledge of history, they saw clearly the settler threat to the African way of life.

The settlers began to fight back in August, after the agreement in Matabeleland. But the war went on for another year. The settler forces burnt fields and houses. There was drought, and people were going hungry. They ate wild roots and berries, and continued to fight. They stored food and water, and hid in caves at night for safety. They fought with great **courage**. The mediums told them that Mwari would turn the settler bullets into water. This was not quite true, but the belief was made stronger by the fact that none of the mediums or chiefs was killed by settler bullets.

The settlers could not get the people to come out of the caves. So they threw explosives into the caves. They killed hundreds of men, women and children. The rest had to give up. Slowly, the people left their caves. The BSAC did not try to talk or reach agreement with the Shona chiefs as they had done in Matabeleland. The paramount chiefs who had joined the uprising were executed or put in prison. Their sons were not allowed to become chiefs in their place. New chiefs were chosen by the Company. They were paid by the Company. They were told what to do by the Company.

Mkwati fled into the north-east, where he died in September 1897. One month later, Kaguvi was captured. Nehanda was arrested in December. Nehanda and Kaguvi were tried by the settler courts. They were hanged on 27 April 1898 in Harare prison. Nehanda died bravely, singing and shouting that her children would return to free the people.

A photo of the Nehanda medium from the First Chimurenga, taken prisoner by the settlers in 1898. She said her children would return to liberate Zimbabwe.

Handing in arms, Serugwe.

VOCABULARY

grievances	— things that are not right, reasons for complaining or protesting.
oppressors	— people who control and exploit others, often by force.
pardoned	— forgiven without punishment.
revolt	— rebel against, rise up to overthrow.
resistance	— opposing, fighting against invaders.
courage	— that which enables you to control fear when faced with danger.

EXERCISES

Summary

Africans living on the plateau soon learned the meaning of _____ ____. Their _____ and _____ were taken. They were forced to pay a _____ Tax of _____ shillings per _____. The people were getting very angry with the way they were treated by the _____. So the Company set up a _____ Department. But their life had changed so much that people rushed into the hills with their _____ when they saw the _____ Commissioner coming. The Company administrator took most of the _____ for a raid into the _____. Then the fighting began in _____ in March _____. It began in Mashonaland in _____.

Questions

1. What was the Hut Tax? How did it change the African way of life?
2. Why did Rhodes want to talk to the *indunas*? Why did they agree to talk to him?
3. Who was Mkwati? Nehanda? Kaguvi?

Discuss

Oppression. The harsh and unjust treatment of people by other people has happened in most parts of the world at different times in history. It still happens in many places today. One of the worst examples of oppression today is in South Africa. Many of the things you have read about in this chapter also happened in South Africa. It was colonized in the interests of imperialism. The land and natural resources were taken. The Africans were pushed onto poorer land. They are still not free. They are forced to work for capitalist companies for little pay. They are forced to live in certain places. They must carry passes showing where they work and where they live. They can be thrown into prison for not carrying their pass. They do not have very many rights. They are not allowed to choose the leaders of their country.

When oppression gets very harsh then the people fight against it as they did in Zimbabwe. What do you think will happen in South Africa?

Project

Ask your grandparents or any old people in your family what stories they know about the 1896-7 war and how people lived then. Then you can tell some of these stories at your next history lesson.

The spirit mediums of Nehanda and Kaguvi were organizers of the First Chimurenga in 1896-7. Nehanda was the sister of Mutota, the first Munhumutapa, who lived more than 500 years ago. Her influence continued through the second war of liberation when the freedom fighters carried another Nehanda medium to their main rear base to advise them in the war.

12 The Settlers Take Control

After the uprising, the British government began to show more interest in the BSA Company and the colony of Rhodesia. In 1898, they passed the Southern Rhodesia Order in Council. This set up a **Legislative** Council to govern the colony. The settlers began to make laws that forced Africans to serve white interests.

Legacy of Disunity

The uprising left a **legacy** of disunity among Africans on the plateau. The existing society was shattered. The Shona chiefs were dead or in prison. The people did not trust the new settler-paid chiefs. Military patrols terrorized the people. The old men had lost hope. The young men had no leadership and took no action.

After some time, things began to change. The crops began to grow again. The trials stopped. The patrols withdrew. The new chiefs began to take over, even though the people were not happy about it. There were often rumours of another uprising. The settlers could replace the chiefs, but they could not choose the spirit mediums. A new medium of Chaminuka appeared and was arrested. A new Nehanda medium was closely watched. Umlugulu had not given up his plan to revive the Ndebele nation, and there were rumours of meetings with Mwari priests. In Mashonaland, the people took their grievances to Kunzwi-Nyandoro. He was the only senior Shona chief who remained in power. The Anglo-Boer War in 1899 and the Anglo-German War in 1914 gave the Africans hope that the British would be defeated. But they were not.

Mapondera returned from Mozambique. He was an old Rozvi chief who had left the Mazoe valley in 1894 to join Makombe of Barwe in fighting against the Portuguese. He had not joined the uprising in his own country. When he returned in 1900, he stayed in the north-east border area near Dande, where the rebellion had not spread. He joined forces with Chioco, the last chief to use the title Munhumutapa. His men were well armed. There was one big battle in Dande early in 1901. There were a few raids on the settlers and their paid chiefs. Resistance continued in the border area until 1917. The Portuguese administration in the Zambezi valley broke down completely that year under a new Shona uprising. It was led by a new Makombe, with the Mutapa mediums Kamota and Dzivaguru. The uprising was crushed by the Portugese. The Africans on the plateau did not take up arms again for more than 40 years.

Early milk delivery, Gweru.

African Reserves

The BSA Company wanted more Europeans in the colony. So it began to sell the land very cheaply. Africans were not allowed to buy it. Grazing land was sold to new settlers for 12 cents an acre, and farm land for 52 cents an acre. But the charter given to the company by the British government said that some land must be kept for Africans. So the Company mapped out areas where Africans would be allowed to farm. They kept the good land for the Europeans. The African areas, called "reserves", were on poor, dry land. The reserves were far away from markets and from the railway line. So it was difficult for African farmers to sell their produce.

Many people were crowded onto poor land. So the land began to suffer. The Africans farmed by shifting cultivation, as we have seen. This allowed the land to rest and prevented soil erosion. Now they were not allowed to move, and the land had no rest. Soil erosion increased. Some African farmers in Mashonaland were allowed to stay on their old land when it served the interest of the settlers. The settlers collected rent from the Africans for using the land. They were close enough to supply food and labour for the settlers. The number of African-owned cattle increased up to 1921 and so did the output of maize. But European farming expanded. Then the settlers wanted those markets to sell their own produce. In 1909, the rent was increased. This forced more African farmers to go to the reserves.

Harare from the kopje, 1900. The settlers named the place after a British government official called Salisbury.

African Labour

The settlers made plans to force Africans to work for them even though the pay was very low. The Hut Tax was increased in 1904. Then each African man had to pay 20 shillings a year. He also had to pay 10 shillings tax for each wife after the first one. So Africans were forced to work for the settlers to make money to pay taxes. This meant that Europeans had to pay less tax. A single European man who made less than $500 a year did not pay any tax at all. A tax on dogs began in 1912. Cattle dipping started in 1914. This cost one or two shillings a head, and was done at the wish of the white farmer. By 1923, most African cattle were being dipped at great cost to their owners

Africans still did not want to work for the settlers. So a Native Labour office was set up in 1903. Many workers came from Northern Rhodesia and Nyasaland. By 1926, more than half the African workers in Southern Rhodesia were from outside the country. Workers who work far away from home are called migrant workers. Many of them worked in the mines where the job was dangerous, the pay was very little, and the living conditions were bad. The settlers tried to get contract workers from In-

First train from Cape Town, 1897.

Missionaries came to Africa as agents of imperialism. They were given large areas of land by the settler government, and they tried to impose their religion on the people. But many missionaries learned about the society they were living in and joined the people's struggle for freedom. They offered education and health care to Africans in the rural areas, and later some gave food and medicine to the freedom fighters.

dia, China and Ethiopia. But working conditions in Southern Rhodesia were so bad that the British government refused to allow them to come.

Master Servant Act

The Master Servant Act of 1901 turned African workers into "short term slaves". If an African left a job before his contract was over, he had to pay a fine or go to prison. He had to pay a fine or go to prison if he did his work "carelessly", or if he was rude to his white boss. The employer was allowed to pay almost nothing, to give little food and poor housing, and to use a *sjambok* to beat the African worker.

Settler Economy

Cheap African labour was the key to the settler economy. Farming and mining took time to develop and make money. But when the settlers came, there was one resource that could be exploited at once. That was African labour.

The settlers used money from African taxes to develop their industry. They also used the extra money they made by paying African workers so little. The railway was built through Rhodesia in 1897. It was built by African labour, and using the **profits** from African labour. But it was owned by the BSA Company. The railway made a lot of money carrying copper from Northern Rhodesia. The coal mine at Hwange was also owned by the BSAC. Another company had a **monopoly** on chrome. A few companies were mining gold. The shares of these companies were held by people outside the country. So most of the money earned was taken out of the country.

Before the settlers came, the people on the plateau made everything they needed. Now they began to buy goods from the settlers' shops. In the past, honey was used to sweeten food. Now they bought sugar. Instead of making clay pots for cooking, they bought metal ones. Instead of twisting grass to make string, they bought string. In the past, traditional tobacco was smoked in pipes. Now they began to buy cigarettes made from tobacco grown on settler farms. In this way, Africans were drawn into the settler economy.

African Education

The nearest Europeans were Christian missionaries. They had not made many converts before 1900, but after that they began to convert more Africans to Christianity. Their mission stations began to offer western medicine and education. But the settlers wanted Africans to learn only enough to do certain jobs. The first education law of 1899 gave the mission schools 10 shillings for each African student. But at least two hours each day had to be spent on industrial training that would be of use to the settler economy.

More and more Africans wanted to go to school. They saw that people with some education got better jobs. They had seen many people cheated because they could not read or write. The settlers built schools for their own children. The mission schools took care of African education.

Settler Government

The Company charter over Southern Rhodesia was extended in 1914. But the settlers no longer wanted Company rule. They wanted their own government. A British legal committee ruled that the land belonged to the British government and not to the Company. So the Company did not want to spend any more money on running the colony. The British government and the Company said Rhodesia should join South Africa. But the settlers opposed this union. The white working class in Rhodesia did not want union. They feared their jobs would be taken by poor whites from the south. They did not like the South African leader, Jan Smuts, because he had broken an armed uprising by white mine workers. The European farmers did not want union either, because African farm workers in the south were paid more money. British settlers in Rhodesia did not want union because they were afraid they would be outnumbered by Afrikaners.

A **referendum** was held in Southern Rhodesia. There were 19 000 European voters. But only 30 Africans were allowed to vote. Voters had to be able to read and write English. Their income had to be more than $135 a year. So most Africans did not qualify. The settlers voted for their own government. Company rule ended in 1923, and the colony became self-governing. This meant that the settlers ran their own affairs. The British government kept power over foreign and African affairs. The local assembly was not allowed to change certain laws, and the British government kept power to make certain laws. All laws relating to **discrimination** against Africans were to be sent to the British government for approval. But the British government never used these powers. No Rhodesian law was refused, and no new laws were offered. This system of government remained until the Review Conference of 1961.

Clark's picture studio, 1906.

VOCABULARY

legislative	—	law-making.
legacy	—	what was left behind afterwards.
profits	—	money gained from business dealings.
monopoly	—	only one allowed to supply.
referendum	—	vote on a political question.
discrimination	—	seeing a difference between, treating differently.

EXERCISES

Summary
The settlers could replace the chiefs but they could not choose the _____ _____. Resistance continued in the border area until _____. The British government passed the _____ _____ Order in Council in _____. This set up a _____ Council to govern the colony. At first most members were chosen by the _____ but this was soon changed to give the _____ more power. The British government and the BSA Company wanted Southern Rhodesia to join with _____ _____. But the settlers wanted _____ _____. They got it in 1923.

Questions
1. Why were African farmers no longer able to use shifting cultivation?
2. How did the settlers force Africans to work for them?
3. What was the Master Servant Act?
4. What are migrant workers?
5. What was the key to the settler economy?

Discuss
The importance of education. We have seen in this chapter that the settlers wanted Africans to be educated only to do certain types of jobs, to use their hands. The settlers wanted their own children to be educated to do other kinds of jobs, to use their heads. In Zimbabwe, we have a new system called Education with Production. This enables us to learn how to use our heads and our hands, to think and to do and to be self-reliant. Why is this type of education important to our new society?

Project
Write down a list of goods you use now that replace traditional items used 100 years ago. Then find different examples of the new and the old to bring to school. Make a small display of these in the classroom.

13 African Protest Movements

Africans continued to **protest** against settler rule in Southern Rhodesia. But they found new ways to do it. The new ways of protest were guided by two things, land and labour. The main grievance was the loss of the land. But contacts with European workers and South African black workers, opened the way for new ideas of protest. The first African protest movements in Southern Rhodesia took four different forms.

Matabele Home Movement

The issues of land and labour were sharpest in Matabeleland. Most land there had been taken by the settlers. In the past, the Ndebele men had looked after the cattle and the war. When both were gone, they moved to the towns to find work. Bulawayo was the economic centre of the country then and there were many jobs.

After the 1896 war, the senior *indunas* had been left in place as leaders of their people. They wanted good land to be set aside in one place and a king restored. They formed the Matabele Home Movement led by Lobengula's son, Nyamanda. They sent letters and appeals to the Company, the settlers, and the British government. But they did not get what they wanted.

Bantu Voters Association

Some Africans from south of the Limpopo River had come to Southern Rhodesia with the settlers. Others came later as part of a Fingo community. They were promised land and rights by Rhodes. They soon found that the land they were given was poor, and they did not have the same rights as whites. But many of these Fingo people were among the 30 Africans allowed to vote in 1923. They formed the Rhodesian Bantu Voters **Association** (RBVA). The leader was Abraham Twala, a Zulu preacher. The main organizer was a woman called Martha Ngano. She was a mission teacher. The RBVA met with the settler government. They tried to get more rights. They tried to get more Africans on the voting role. But they were a small group who did not have much support among the people.

Union of Workers

The Rhodesian Industrial and Commercial Workers **Union** (RICU) was the first movement to unite workers in the city. It was formed in 1927. Other movements supported the British government and the Church. But the RICU did not do this. The RICU wanted African **urban** workers to forget regional differences and unite to demand better working conditions. The RICU organizer in Bulawayo was Shona, while the organizer in Harare was Ndebele.

Some Africans came with the settlers.

All of these movements got help from Africans in South Africa. Those who wanted to vote got ideas from J.T. Jabavu in the Cape. Those who wanted to protest were advised by the Communist Party of South Africa and the African National Congress. The RICU got ideas from migrant workers from all over southern Africa. The leader of the same union in South Africa, the ICU, was Clemens Kadalie. He was from Nyasaland. He worked for a mining company in Southern Rhodesia before he went to South Africa. Workers in Southern Rhodesia asked him for help in organizing the RICU. The RICU leaders were Charles Mzingeli and Masotsha Ndlovu. They had been migrant workers in South Africa, where there were black trade unions and the wages were higher.

African Churches

The trade union movement took a long time to organize workers in Southern Rhodesia because there was no African working class. The urban workers were people who had been forced off their land. They wanted to return to the land. They did not want to stay in the city. The most popular protest movement at that time was based in the **rural** areas. This was the African churches. The African churches used both religion and politics. They were against settler rule. They protested against the loss of land and the exploiting of labour. They spoke against settler laws. They gave Africans hope for the future. Some of the leaders of these African churches were Rev. M.D. Makgatho and Matthew Chagaga Zvimba.

Land Apportionment Act

Apportionment means divide or distribute. The dividing of the land became law under the Land Apportionment Act of 1931. There were many more Africans than Europeans living in Southern Rhodesia. But the Europeans got 49 million acres. This was more than half the land. And it was the best land for farming or grazing. The poor land was made into African "reserves". This was 21½ million acres. Another 7½ million acres became "purchase areas", where Africans were allowed to buy small areas of land. But most Africans did not have money to buy land. The other 18 million acres were very poor land and were later added to the African areas.

Bantu Congress

The settler government did not listen to African protests. So the African churches got even more support. Then Africans in the European churches formed their own association. This was separate from the white Missionary Conference. But the African Conference had little power. Anything it wanted to do had to be approved by the Europeans. It was not allowed to speak against the Land Apportionment Act. Some of its

A recent picture of Masotsha Ndlovu, who started RICU with Charles Mzingeli.

A meeting of the Bantu Congress, formed in 1934, later called the African National Congress.

leaders, such as Rev. Thompson Samkange and Rev. Matthew Rusike, formed the Bantu Congress in 1934. It was led by Aaron Jacha, a purchase area farmer.

War in Europe

During the 1930s, there was a depression in Europe and America. That meant that there was not very much money, and many businesses closed down. Many people lost their jobs. This spread to the colonies. But things changed when war broke out in Europe in 1939. The colonial powers needed men and minerals to fight the war. The mines and industry in Southern Rhodesia expanded. Thousands more Africans were needed to work at jobs in the cities. Thousands of others were recruited to fight in the British war against Germany and Japan. African soldiers fought on the same side as European soldiers. They shared the same hardships, the same fears and the same pain. Many died together. But when the African soldiers returned home after the war, they were treated badly. They were sent back to the reserves. European soldiers and new settlers were given money to buy farms. This happened in many African countries. It made the African soldiers very angry. Many of them were active in forming **nationalist** movements to work for the freedom of their people.

African Voice

In Southern Rhodesia, the African National Congress was started by Rev. Samkange and other leaders from the old Bantu Congress. But the settlers would not listen to them. The trade unions had more power than political parties in the years right after the war.

The Reformed Industrial and Commercial Union was started again by Mzingeli and Ndlovu. Another trade union in Bulawayo organized African butchers, bakers, shopkeepers and others. Benjamin Burombo said this was helping the rich, not the working class. So he broke away and formed the British African Voice Association. The Rhodesian Railways African Employees Association in Bulawayo organized a **strike** of railway workers in 1945. It spread to other railway centres and lasted two weeks. Then Burombo's Voice Association and others helped to organize the first general, or national, strike by African workers. It began on 14 April 1948 and spread to every urban area and mining centre in the country. The settlers did not know what to do. African workers were demanding more money, better housing, and better working conditions. The government spoke of change and the workers went back to work. Labour boards were set up to look into African wages. But there were few real changes.

The Rhodesian African Rifles in Burma during the war of 1939-45.

Benjamin Burombo was a big man, well over six feet tall. He organized the people to fight against oppression and he inspired many young nationalists who came after him.

Land Husbandry Act

The oppression got worse with the Land Husbandry Act of 1951. Husbandry means the use of land for farming. This Act meant that the chiefs could not distribute land. A father could not pass on his land to his children. The land could be sold but not divided. Farmers could stay on the land only if they farmed in a certain way. The Act also ended any right to land by urban workers. Its aim was to divide African small farmers from the workers, and to push more Africans into the cities to work for the settlers. Between 1946 and 1953, half a million Africans moved from rural to urban areas.

Burombo's Voice Association led the protest against the Land Husbandry Act. The Voice dealt with grievances in both urban and rural areas. It tried to unite the workers and small farmers, called peasants. Burombo was a very fine speaker in Ndebele and Shona. He was against tribalism and for unity. He told Africans that the riches they saw around them came from the use of their labour. He told people they must liberate themselves, and he gave them hope that they could do it.

The Land Husbandry Act forced Africans to sell their cattle at low prices. Each family was limited to five cows and eight acres of land. A story told by one young boy shows how angry people were with this law. His father gave him one cow. He looked after it together with the rest of his father's cattle. But the new law forced his father to sell most of his cattle including the son's cow. When the father came back from the market, he gave his son one shilling, even though the cow was worth much more. He put the shilling into a pot. Every day he told the boy to look into the pot and see if there was more than one shilling. Each day the boy replied there was not. After some time the father told the son the shilling had not increased because they were oppressed. The cow now belonged to a white man. It was producing calves for the white man. But the shilling paid by the white man would never reproduce. The father said the law was to keep Africans poor while the whites got rich.

VOCABULARY

protest	—	to speak or fight against something.
association	—	group of people who meet to decide how to do certain things.
union	—	unity of workers.
urban	—	having to do with the city.
rural	—	having to do with the countryside outside the cities.
nationalist	—	person who supports political and economic freedom for his/her country.
strike	—	when workers refuse to work until their demands are met.

EXERCISES

Summary

The Land _____ Act was passed in _____. There were more _____ than _____ living in Southern Rhodesia, but the _____ were given more than half of the land. The poor land was made into African _____ or _____ _____. The Land _____ Act was passed 20 years later, in _____. Then the chiefs could no longer distribute _____. A father could not give _____ to his children. The _____ could be sold but not divided. Each family was limited to _____ cows and eight acres of _____. _____ workers no longer had rights to _____. The aim was to divide the African small farmers, called _____, and the workers.

Questions

1. Why did the trade union movement have difficulty organizing people in the 1920s and 1930s?
2. Why were African soldiers angry when they came back from the war in Europe?
3. What is the difference between a protest movement, a nationalist movement, and a trade union?

Discuss

Money and wealth. How did the Europeans in Southern Rhodesia get rich while most Africans did not? How was land and labour used to do this? How was law used? For example, how did the Europeans get the best land? What was the effect of the law restricting Africans to a few acres of land and a few cattle? How were urban workers exploited?

The Land Apportionment Act. 1931

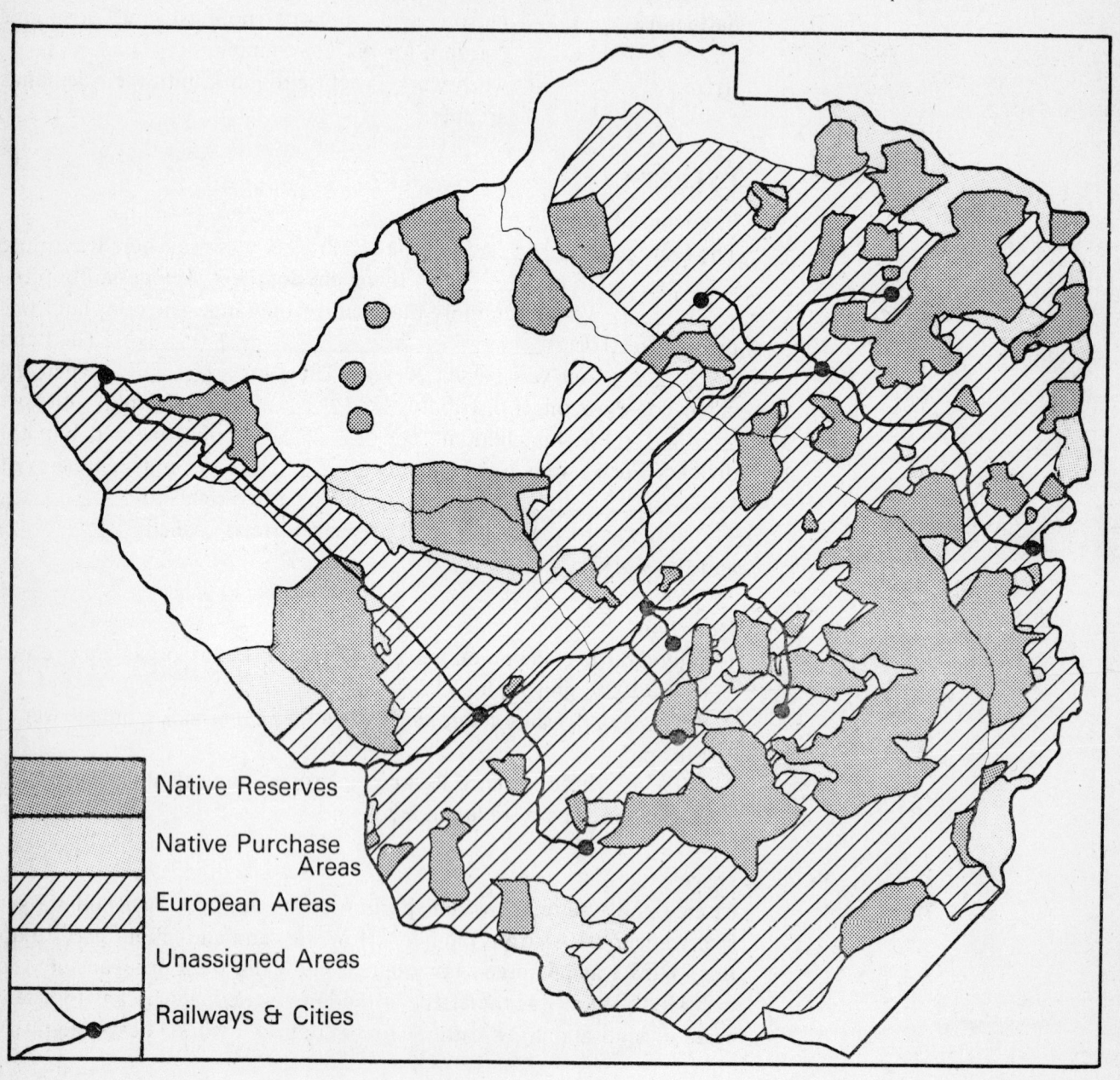

Project

Many people in Zimbabwe, of all ethnic backgrounds, work with the railways. Organize a visit for the students to the nearest railway station, or railway siding. Learn how the railways work, and what jobs people do on the railways. If your school is too far away to visit the railway, then try to find someone who can come to your school and talk about railways. Or write a letter to the nearest railway station, or the Ministry of Transport in Harare. Ask for information and pictures.

Legend:
- Native Reserves
- Native Purchase Areas
- European Areas
- Unassigned Areas
- Railways & Cities

14 The Settler Colonial State

African labour was the key to the settler economy in Southern Rhodesia. Most laws passed by the settler government were made to control African labour. There were laws over land, cattle, education, health, wages, where to live, and even where an African could be at any time. An African's life was ruled by the part he or she played in the settler colonial state.

"Native" Legislation

Every African man over 14 years of age had to carry a card saying who he was and where he came from. If he was caught without his card he was put in prison. If he was found in town without work he could be forced to work. The "Native" Registration Act of 1936 forced him to carry a pass to prove he worked in town, or had **permission** to look for work in town. The Native (Urban Areas) **Accommodation** Act of 1946 set up locations near the towns where Africans could live. An African board could offer ideas to the white city council about roads or beerhalls in the township. The word "native" was later taken out of laws and replaced with "African". In 1962, the "Native" Department became the Department of Internal Affairs.

Education

Education was made compulsory for whites, coloureds and Asians in 1930. That meant all non-black children had to go to school. Education was not compulsory for Africans. The settler government was afraid that educated Africans would want more rights. White workers were afraid that educated Africans would take their jobs. The Public Services Act was passed in 1931 to stop non-whites from joining the civil service except as teachers or nurses. The Industrial Conciliation Act was passed in 1934 to protect white workers. Africans could not be counted as workers and could not form trade unions.

Between 1929 and 1943, the settler government worked against African education. The number of schools and students dropped. The only government schools for Africans were two trade schools. The only non-Africans helping African education were missionaries. The government took over African education in the cities in 1946. The first government secondary school for Africans was built that year at Goromonzi, near Harare. Two more African secondary schools opened in Bulawayo three years later. But African children who went to school between 1933 and 1950 went mostly because of their parents. Parents would spend the little money they had to educate at least one of their children. Most mission schools were in the rural areas, and the parents often made the bricks to build the schools. The parents paid for books, pencils and rulers, as well

Oppressive legislation controlled the lives of Africans in Southern Rhodesia.

Most African children could not go to school. There were too few schools and the fees were too high. Their parents often went without food so they had money to send one child to school.

as fees. Often the parents went without food or extra clothing to pay for a child's education.

Labour

The capitalists who owned the mines and factories wanted African workers with some education or training. They wanted Africans to take some of the **skilled** jobs. They knew they could pay African workers less money than whites. They could pay a few white workers a high salary only if there were many Africans working at a low salary. During the war in Europe, 1939 - 1945, more Africans moved into skilled jobs when many white workers were out of the country. Then the capitalists began to see that they would get more and better work if the African men were allowed to live in town. So the government passed the 1946 act that created locations. Before this, African men who worked in the city stayed in compounds with many other men. Their families stayed in the rural areas. The employers often said these men did not need much pay because their wives made a living working on the land.

Poverty

In 1948 Africans working in urban areas were paid only four dollars a month, including food. This was well below the **Poverty** Datum Line (PDL). The PDL is information used to find out what is the least amount of money needed to live. In 1943, the least amount for a single African man to live was just over six dollars. For a family, it was ten dollars. A study in 1953 showed that more than half of the African families living in the cities did not have enough money to live on.

African workers began to get angry when their children were going without food, and when they were doing the same job as whites for much less pay. The European doing the same job often made ten times as much as the African. The first African trade union allowed by the settler government was the Railway Workers Union in 1949, after the strike. Africans in most other trades were not allowed to form unions until 10 years later. Africans working on European farms or in European houses were never allowed to form trade unions. They had no fixed wage, very poor housing, and little time off.

Health

African workers paid taxes, as we have seen. But the settler government spent most of this money in the cities. Most of the money for health was spent in urban areas and on hospitals for whites only. African health care was very poor. It was designed to fit the needs of the settler economy, to prevent the spread of smallpox and other diseases, and to create healthy African workers for the mines and factories. Fever hospitals and mine hospitals were built. But most hospitals in rural areas were set up by missionaries. Most sickness in the rural areas was related to poor living conditions.

The settlers built schools for their children like the ones in Europe and taught European education. All white children had to go to school.

Many women had to stay on the land while the men went to towns to find work.

Racial Discrimination

Discrimination by race occurred in all areas of life. What we have studied about land, labour, education and health applied to housing, social welfare, small businesses and bank loans. Africans were refused entry to hotels, restaurants, public toilets, and public areas on railways. Swimming pools and bars were strictly **segregated**. It was against the law for an African to drink European beer before 1957, and to drink spirits before 1959.

A series of laws controlled African protests against these conditions. The Native Affairs Act in 1928. The **Sedition** Act in 1936. The **Subversive** Activities Act in 1950. The Public Order Act in 1955. The Law and Order Act in 1960.

Early Settler Politics

The settlers did not always agree about how to deal with Africans, as we have seen. The company owners, or capitalists, wanted to use cheap African labour and make more profits. But white workers were afraid of losing their jobs. The largest group of white workers was in the railways. They formed their first union in 1916. Some white workers formed a Labour Party. But the Labour Party broke up in the late 1940s when its members could not agree to include African workers.

This conflict between white labour and capital continued through 10 years of Rhodesia Party government, 1923-33, led by Sir Charles Coghlan and then Howard Moffat. The Rhodesia Party under Moffat agreed to some African development. So it was defeated by white voters in the 1933 election. The Reform Party, led by Godfrey Huggins, was elected because he promised "separate development" for the races. In South Africa, this is called *apartheid* and is still the policy of the white government there. In 1934, Huggins and others broke away from the Reform Party. They joined some members of the Rhodesia Party and formed the United Party. It joined different white classes through their fear of African development. It ruled Southern Rhodesia until 1962.

After the war in Europe, white workers felt threatened by the increase in skilled African labour. So the Southern Rhodesia government recruited more settlers from Europe. By 1953, the white population was 158 000. That was almost double the figure for 1945.

There were many places in the city where Africans were not allowed to go.

VOCABULARY

permission	—	asking and being allowed to do something.
accommodation	—	place for visitors to stay.
skilled	—	having special training to do a certain job.
poverty	—	being very, very poor, without enough money to live.
segregated	—	kept apart, separated by race.
sedition	—	words or actions used to make people disobey the government.
subversive	—	wanted to destroy or overthrow a government.

EXERCISES

Summary

African _____ was the key to the settler economy. An African's life was ruled by the part he or she played in the _____ _____ _____. African men over _____ years of age had to carry a pass. Africans working in urban areas in 1948 were paid only _____ dollars a month. They began to get very angry when their children were going without _____, and when they were doing the same jobs for much less _____ than Europeans. The European doing the same job often earned _____ times as much as the African. The first African trade union was the _____ Workers Union in 1949.

Questions

1. Why was education compulsory for white, coloured and Asian children but not for African children?
2. What is the meaning of Poverty Datum Line?
3. What kind of discrimination did Africans face?
4. Who was Godfrey Huggins and what did he promise?

Discuss

Rules and laws. How were laws used to oppress people in the settler colonial state? Why did so many laws need to be changed after Zimbabwe became independent? What are some of the laws you have seen in this chapter which needed changing? Why?

Project

Ask your father or mother to tell you a story about how one of these laws affected them. Bring this story to school and tell it to the other students.

15 The Failure of Partnership

Industry in Southern Rhodesia continued to grow after the war in Europe. Factory owners began to look outside the country for markets and raw materials. The closest place was across the Zambezi River in Northern Rhodesia. It had copper and other minerals, and a settler community. Northern Rhodesia was ruled directly from Britain. The settlers there were starting to worry about British statements on "native" rights. So settlers from the two countries met in 1949 to discuss their future. Nyasaland did not have mineral wealth or many settlers. But British government said settlers from there should attend the talks. They agreed on a **federation** of the three colonies. They met in London in 1951 and again at Victoria Falls a few months later.

African Opposition

Africans in the two northern colonies did not want federation. They knew of the racial laws in Southern Rhodesia. Many had suffered them as migrant workers. They were getting more rights under direct rule, and they feared a setback. So Harry Nkumbula, leader of the Northern Rhodesia ANC, organized a meeting of Africans from the three countries in 1951. The meeting agreed to oppose the Federation.

Federation

Most settlers in Southern Rhodesia wanted federation with Northern Rhodesia and Nyasaland. They thought they would pay less taxes. That was true, because the federal government got most of its taxes from the sale of Northern Rhodesia's copper. Some settlers in Southern Rhodesia argued against federation. They did not like the idea of bringing together Africans from the three colonies. So there was a referendum in Southern Rhodesia in 1953. More than 25 000 whites voted for federation. About 14 000 voted against. The Federation of Rhodesia and Nyasaland began in September 1953. Godfrey Huggins resigned as Prime Minister of Southern Rhodesia. He became Prime Minister of the Federation. Garfield Todd became Prime Minister of Southern Rhodesia.

The settlers in the three colonies had 26 seats in the Federal Parliament. The Africans had six, even though there were many more Africans than Europeans. Most of the voters were white. Fewer than 450 Africans in Southern Rhodesia were allowed to vote. The amount of money a person had to earn in a year to get on the voters' roll had been doubled, to over $300, to prevent more Africans from voting.

Many Africans in Southern Rhodesia hoped that the federation would help them to get the same rights as Africans in the other two colonies.

Godfrey Huggins, later Lord Malvern. He was Prime Minister of Southern Rhodesia for 20 years. He promised "separate development" and said Africans should not be in government for a very long time.

That was not much, but it was more than they had. The African members in the federal parliament from the other two colonies spoke out against colonial rule. They spoke in favour of African rights. Africans in Southern Rhodesia wanted their members to do the same.

Liberal Hopes

Some African leaders in Southern Rhodesia thought the settlers would work with them in a kind of **partnership** if they took time to explain African views. Some educated Africans played this role for a time. They moved among **liberal** whites. They talked about political, economic and social rights for Africans. But they still had laws that told them where they could live, eat and drink.

A few liberal whites worked for better race relations. They worked by themselves. Or in groups such as the Capricorn Africa Society and the United Club. They wanted changes, but not always as much or as fast as the Africans wanted. In Britain, a group called the Fabian Society urged the government to improve the life of people in the colonies.

Another group that tried to bring Africans and Europeans together was the Inter-Racial Association. They held small parties where Africans and Europeans could meet, talk, and have a drink, even though this was against the law. They prepared information that led to changes in some laws, such as the Liqour Act. The word "native" was removed from laws. Some African workers were finally allowed to form trade unions in 1959.

But most of the settlers, civil servants and politicians ignored them. They were only a small pressure group and had no power in parliament. They were talking to the same whites who already agreed with what they were doing.

Garfield Todd

These Africans and liberal whites worked closely with Todd, who was then Prime Minister. Todd believed in talking with African leaders. He made many liberal statements. His Five-Year Education Plan put more African children into schools and gave more pay to African teachers. He once said he would resign unless more Africans, such as teachers and nurses, were added to the voters' roll.

But other white leaders thought things were changing too fast. Huggins said an African role in government was something to be decided by "our grandchildren". Most settlers did not like what Todd was saying, and he was removed by his own party. Edgar Whitehead replaced him as SR Prime Minister in 1958. Todd formed another party, the Central African Party.

African leaders in all three countries opposed the Federation. Few Africans accepted the six seats in the federal parliament where they had no power.

Garfield Todd was prime minister after Huggins. White Rhodesians thought he was changing things too fast.

Edson Sithole.

James Chikerema.

George Nyandoro.

Joshua Nkomo.

City Youth League

Many Africans thought changes were taking too long. So they formed the City Youth League in 1955. This was led by James Chikerema, George Nyandoro, Edson Sithole and Dunduzu Chisiza from Nyasaland, who was later sent back by Todd. Chisiza believed that Africans in the three colonies must unite to fight against federation. The CYL was more **militant** than earlier groups. The leaders spoke against settler rule. They wanted **majority rule**. They were opposed to African members in a federal parliament. They had lost hope in the Inter-Racial Association. In 1956, they organized a protest against high bus fares. Africans refused to use buses for three days. The CYL got their members elected to the African Boards in the townships which could advise on street lights and beerhalls.

African National Congress

The Bulawayo branch of the ANC had kept going after federation. Jason Moyo, Joseph Msika and others organized meetings and spoke about African grievances. In 1957, they joined with the CYL leaders to make the ANC a national organization. This was 12 September, the same day as the settlers were celebrating "occupation day". ANC members met in Harare and made Joshua Nkomo the president and James Chikerema the vice-president. Nkomo was a social worker with the railways. He was general secretary of the Railways African Workers Union, and then chairman of the Trade Union Congress.

The new ANC gained support in urban and rural areas. It opposed racial laws on land. It sent Africans out of the country to study. It's motto was "Forward ever, backward never". In 1958 the nationalist parties were busy in all three colonies. In 1959, they were **banned**. In Southern Rhodesian, a State of Emergency was declared. That meant the government could take any action to keep the peace. More than 500 Africans were arrested, including most ANC leaders. Nkomo was out of the country. But the others were kept in prison for three years. The white minority government had shown that it would not listen to anyone, black or white, who wanted majority rule.

VOCABULARY

federation	—	a political system in which each state controls its own affairs but leaves foreign affairs, defence, and so on, to a central government.
partnership	—	working together.
liberal	—	free from prejudice, in favour of some changes.
militant	—	willing to speak out or fight for a cause.
majority rule	—	when each adult has one vote and the party that wins the election forms the government. Majority means more than half. Minority means a few.
banned	—	not allowed to meet.

EXERCISES

Summary

The Federation of _____ and _____ was formed in _____. The Prime Minister was _____. The new Prime Minister of Southern Rhodesia was _____. In the federal parliament there were _____ seats for whites and _____ seats for Africans. They were elected by the white voters. Fewer than _____ Africans were allowed to vote. The amount of money a person had to earn in a year to get on the voters' roll had been doubled to _____ to stop more Africans from voting. Some African workers were finally allowed to form trade unions in _____.

Questions

1. Why were Africans in Northern Rhodesia and Nyasaland opposed to federation?
2. What was the City Youth league and why was it formed?
3. Why did CYL leaders later join with ANC leaders?

Discuss

Living together without prejudice. We have seen in this chapter how some Africans and Europeans talked to each other, became friends, and tried to work out their problems together. They had no prejudice. But they were prevented by the laws. Now those laws have been changed. How can we live and work together without prejudice as to race, colour, sex, wealth or religion?

Project

Try to find a man or woman in your district who was active during the Federation. This may be a relative or friend of one of the students, or someone known by the teacher. Invite this person to come to the school and talk to the students. Ask him or her what are the most important things that have changed since that time.

The Federation of Rhodesia and Nyasaland, 1953-63

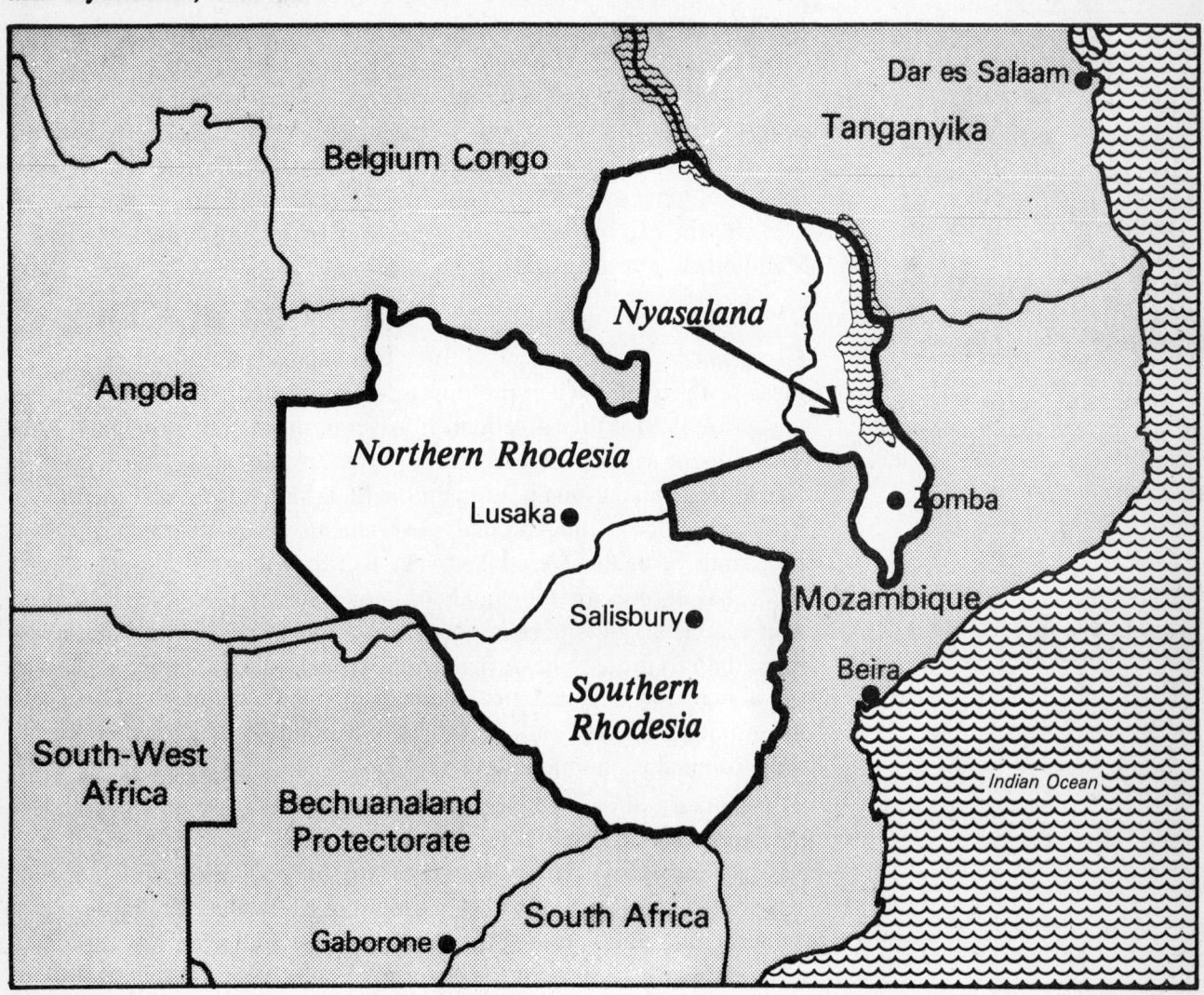

16 Growth of African Nationalism

In 1956, only four countries in all of Africa were free of colonial rule. Ethiopia had been independent throughout its history, except for a few years when it was occupied by Italy. Liberia had been independent since 1847, Egypt since 1922, and Libya since 1953.

On 6 March 1957, the Gold Coast became independent as Ghana, led by Kwame Nkrumah. Nkrumah **inspired** nationalists in many African countries with his ideas about freedom from colonial rule. He believed that Africans must be united. He held an All-African People's Conference in Ghana in 1958. Many African leaders met there for the first time. By the end of 1961, there were 26 independent African countries. Many others got independence in 1963 and 1964.

Kwame Nkrumah, the first president of Ghana. He inspired many African leaders with his ideas about freedom from colonial rule.

"The Wind of Change"

Governments in Europe were forced to change some of their colonial ideas in the 1950s, when the oppressed people in some of the colonies began to fight for their freedom. In Algeria, the people formed the FLN. They fought against the French for more than seven years, and won. In Kenya, African nationalists fought the Mau Mau war against the British. These wars cost the colonial governments a lot of money. Many thousands of people were killed. The British, French and other governments began to see that it would cost money and lives to keep the empire as it was. It became more important to **protect** British trade and **investment** than to protect the settlers from African rule. So imperialism took on a new form, called neo-colonialism. That means that European governments tried to choose African governments which would protect their colonial economic interests.

In January 1960, the British Minister, Harold Macmillan, made a famous speech in Cape Town. He spoke of the "wind of change" that was blowing across Africa. He meant that independence was spreading across Africa. He was warning the white settlers that they must accept majority rule. But south of the Zambezi River, the wind was blowing a different way. In Southern Rhodesia and South Africa, the white minority governments refused to give Africans their rights.

National Democratic Party

New African parties were formed in the Federation in place of those which were banned. The Malawi Congress Party was formed in Nyasaland. The United National Independence Party was formed in Northern Rhodesia. On 1 January 1960, Africans in Southern Rhodesia formed the National Democratic Party (NDP) which became the voice of

African nationalism. It was formed by African leaders who were not in prison. Among them were Enos Nkala, Sketchley Samkange, George Silundika, and Leopold Takawira. Michael Mawema was made president for a time, until Nkomo returned from Europe later in the year. He had spent 20 months touring the world getting support. He was made director of external affairs, and then president. The problems of Africans in Southern Rhodesia were not well known outside the country. The NDP members hoped that Nkomo's contacts in Europe, Asia and America would help them to get support. He was chosen at a party congress in October, **when Robert Mugabe also joined the NDP leadership. Mugabe had studied at Fort Hare University in South Africa, and had just returned from teaching in Ghana. He was a popular speaker at rallies. He told the people about *apartheid* in South Africa. He told them about Nkrumah and freedom in Ghana, where Africans were ruling themselves.**

At this time, Whitehead was asking the British government to give more power to the settler government in Southern Rhodesia. The NDP worked against this. They sent some members to London to meet the Commonwealth Secretary. Later, they opened an office in London. One of the aims of the NDP was to educate the British people. So Takawira and Moton Malianga went on a speaking tour in Britain. They told the people it was not true that Southern Rhodesia was independent and that Africans had a better life there than in other African countries.

Nkomo, in a traditional hat worn by some nationalists at that time, and George Silundika, secretary-general of the NDP.

Robert Mugabe, who had just returned from Ghana, and Leopold Takawira, a founder member of the NDP and a teacher who inspired many of his students to oppose the oppression of settler rule.

July 1960

The NDP wanted changes in the **constitution**. They wanted majority rule. Takawira wrote: "We are no longer asking Europeans to rule us well. We now want to rule ourselves." In July 1960, Takawira and two others were arrested. Their houses and party offices were searched. Nkala and Silundika led a crowd of 7 000 Africans to protest. They decided to march from Highfield into Harare. They started at midnight, but 500 police stopped them from entering the city. They slept outside and ate food brought by relatives. They were told that Whitehead would meet their leaders. But in the morning he refused. Few Africans went to work in Harare that day. Most joined the marchers. The crowd grew to about 40 000. They stayed quietly waiting outside the city boundary. Then Whitehead ordered the police to break up the crowd. The police began beating people. The people began to throw stones. Soon the streets were littered with broken glass. A bank was broken into. A hotel was damaged. A van was overturned. Three people had gunshot wounds, and 126 people were arrested. The next weekend the fighting spread to Bulawayo. Eleven Africans were killed there. Property damage was more than $130 000. It was the angriest display of African protest since 1896.

Law and Order

The settler government passed new laws giving it more power to arrest anyone who demanded equal rights for Africans. Most important was the Law and Order Act of 1960. The Chief Justice of the Federation, Sir Robert Tredgold, called the new law "evil". He resigned in protest. Other white officials also advised the government to listen to African grievances. But the settlers refused.

1961 Constitution

The British government sent a group of people, called a **commission**, to visit the three colonies. The commission told the British government that it should end the Federation, or give Africans more say in it. So a Federal Review Conference was held in London. But the African nationalist leaders walked out. In January 1961, talks about a Southern Rhodesia constitution began in Harare. The British proposed a new constitution which allowed a few Africans to vote for 15 members of parliament, while Europeans would elect 50 members of parliament. Africans still could not vote unless they had a certain amount of education and money. Those allowed to vote were not as poor as most Africans, but not as rich as most settlers. They formed a kind of middle class, which would support the minority government in exchange for certain **privileges**, such as the vote.

White voters accepted the new constitution. Nkomo also accepted it at first, just as he had done at the time of the Federation. But Takawira sent an angry telegram from London, where he was at the talks on Northern Rhodesia. He said such an agreement was an insult to Southern Rhodesia's three million Africans. The NDP leaders met for four hours. They agreed to reject the proposals on voting. Then they organized a **boycott,** and most African voters refused to vote. But the constitution was accepted because the Europeans voted for it.

Organizing the People

NDP leaders continued to organize the people. Nkomo wanted a general strike. But workers in the cities were afraid of losing their jobs and their housing. They had no rights to land in the rural areas and no rural home to go back to. There were always lines of men with no jobs waiting outside the factories. They were ready to take the places of workers who went on strike.

In the rural areas, people began to destroy things built by the settler government — dip tanks, beer gardens, some schools and teachers' houses. In the cities, there were boycotts of beer and other items that could make industry see there was a problem. This created **solidarity** among the African people. Their leaders told them to have pride in their culture. They told the people to respect their customs, names, music, dances, dress, religion and food. There were thudding drums at NDP meetings and singing and dancing. Water was served in traditional pots. People were asked to take off their shoes, ties, and jackets. This was a symbol of rejecting colonial rule. Mugabe told the last NDP meeting in Highfield: "Today you have removed your shoes. Tomorrow you may be called upon to destroy them altogether, or to perform other acts of self-denial. If European-owned industries are used to buy guns which are aimed against us, we must withdraw our labour and destroy those industries". Mugabe was the NDP secretary for information and publicity. He organized the youth to play a larger role in party activities. They went from house to house in the townships to invite people to meetings. They often led the singing at meetings. Some were sent outside the country for education. A few were sent out for military training.

Mugabe was a popular speaker at meetings and rallies. He spoke of freedom in Ghana and *apartheid* in South Africa. He organized the youth to play a role in party activities and to prepare to fight for freedom.

VOCABULARY

inspired	—	gave hope and direction.
protect	—	keep safe, look after.
investment	—	money put into business to make more money.
constitution	—	laws that say how a country is governed.
commission	—	group of people who study a problem and make suggestions.
privileges	—	special favours given to some people but not to others.
boycott	—	refusal to have anything to do with something until demands are met.
solidarity	—	unity of people working together for something they believe in.

EXERCISES

Summary

In 1956, only four African countries were free from colonial rule. They were _____, _____, _____ and _____. On 6 March _____, the Gold Coast became independent as _____, led by _____ _____. By the end of 1961, there were _____ independent African countries. The British Prime Minister _____ _____ made a famous speech in _____ _____ in 1960. He spoke of the _____ _____. He meant that _____ was spreading across Africa. On 1 January _____, Africans in Southern Rhodesia formed the _____ _____ _____. It became the voice of African _____.

Questions

1. Who was Kwame Nkrumah and how did he inspire African nationalists?
2. Why did the NDP leaders oppose the 1961 constitution?
3. What was the role of the youth in the NDP?

Discuss

Why did Africans want to rule themselves? Why did they want to be free of colonial rule? Why did they want majority rule?

1. Ethiopia, independent throughout
2. Liberia, 26 July 1847
3. Egypt, 28 February 1922
4. Libya, 24 December 1951
5. Sudan, 1 January 1956
6. Morocco, 2 March 1956
7. Tunisia, 20 March 1956
8. Ghana, 6 March 1957
9. Guinea, 28 September 1958
10. Cameroun, 1 January 1960
11. Togo, 27 April 1960
12. Malagasy, 26 June 1960
13. Zaire, 30 June 1960
14. Somalia, 1 July 1960
15. Benin, 1 August 1960
16. Niger, 3 August 1960
17. Upper Volta, 5 August 1960
18. Ivory Coast, 7 August 1960
19. Chad, 11 August 1960
20. Central African Republic, 13 August 1960
21. Congo, 15 August 1960
22. Gabon, 17 August 1960
23. Senegal, 25 August 1960
24. Mali, 22 September 1960
25. Nigeria, 1 October 1960
26. Mauritania, 28 November 1960
27. Sierra Leone, 27 April 1961
28. Tanzania, 9 December 1961
29. Burundi, 1 July 1962
30. Rwanda, 1 July 1962
31. Algeria, 5 July 1962
32. Uganda, 9 October 1962
33. Kenya, 12 December 1963
34. Malawi, 6 July 1964
35. Zambia, 24 October 1964
36. Gambia, 18 February 1965
37. Botswana, 30 September 1966
38. Lesotho, 4 October 1966
39. Mauritius, 12 March 1968
40. Swaziland, 6 September 1968
41. Equatorial Guinea, 12 October 1968
42. Guinea Bissau, 24 September 1973
43. Mozambique, 25 June 1975
44. Cape Verde, 5 July 1975
45. Comoro Island, 6 July 1975
46. Sao Tome & Principe, 12 July 1975
47. Angola, 11 November 1975
48. Seychelles, 28 June 1976
49. Djibouti, 27 June 1977
50. Zimbabwe, 18 April 1980
51. Saharawi
52. Namibia
53. South Africa

Wind of Change

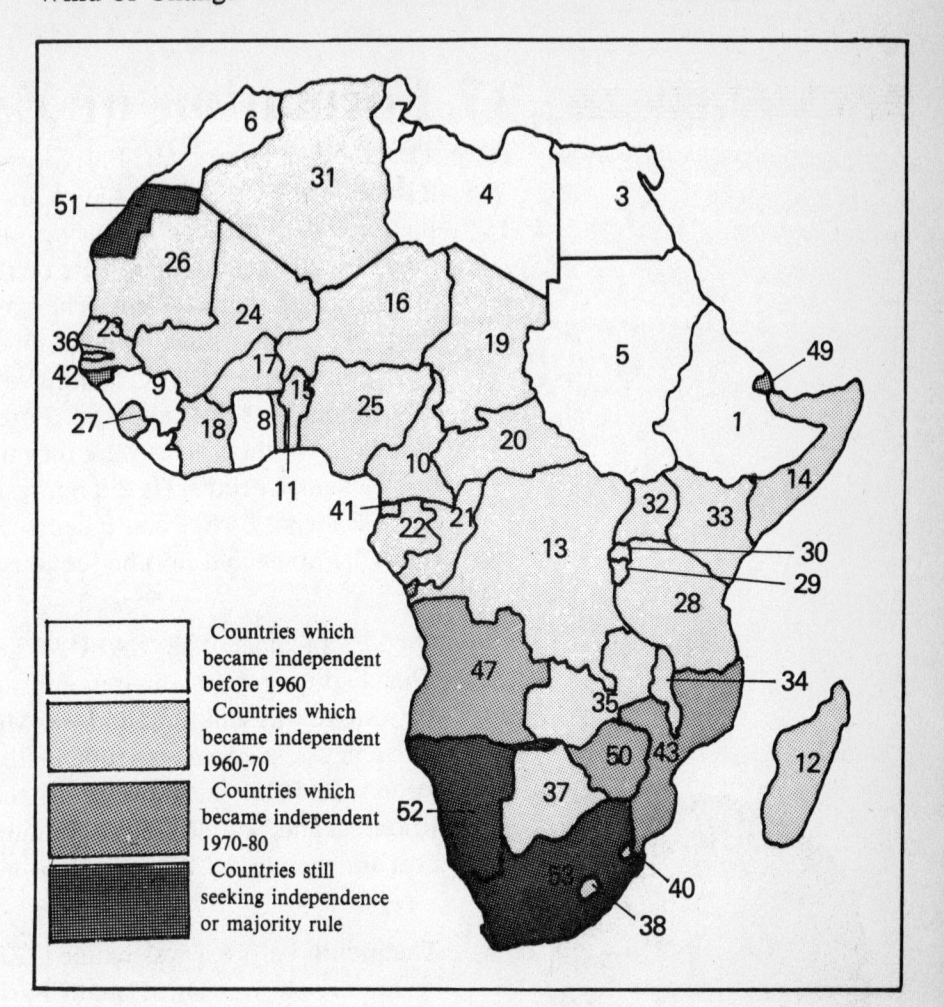

Project

Look at the map in this chapter titled "Wind of Change". It shows you the other countries in Africa. Choose one country. Write to the Ministry of Education there. Ask them to pass on the letter to a school in their country. Tell them what grade you are and what country. Make sure you give them the postal address of your school. The country you choose to write to can be far away like Algeria, Ethiopia, Ghana or Tanzania. Or it can be nearby like Botswana, Malawi, Mozambique, or Zambia.

Ask the students in the school in that country a lot of questions so you can find out how they live. Ask them about their names, customs, music and dances. Ask them about what clothes they wear and what food they eat. Ask them how their country got its independence. Ask them to send you some pictures of their country. Or maybe they could draw some pictures of how they live. Send them some of the same information about yourselves. You could also send some pictures or drawings.

17 Formation of ZAPU and ZANU

The National Democratic Party was banned by the settler government on 9 December 1961. Ten days later, the NDP leaders formed another party, the Zimbabwe African People's Union (ZAPU). Mugabe, Nkala, Silundika, Takawira and others were on the **executive** committee. Again, they made Nkomo the president. Their aims were to work for unity and majority rule, and against colonialism and imperialism.

The members of ZAPU continued the actions of the NDP. The people carried out acts of **sabotage**. Forests were burned. Dip tanks were destroyed. Railway lines were torn up. Many of these acts were ordered by "General Chedu". He did not really exist. It was a name used by some party leaders. ZAPU continued to spread information about African rights, at home and in other countries.

Leaders Restricted

On 20 September 1962, ZAPU was banned. The leaders were **restricted**. They had to stay for three months at small reserves far from the cities. J.Z. Moyo was sent to Somukwe, Mugabe to Makwiro, and Takawira to Mberengwa. Nkomo was not in the country. But African nationalist leaders told him he must return home. So he returned to Southern Rhodesia and was also sent to Somukwe. From there he tried to get support for the idea of a **government-in-exile**.

Parirenyatwa

The month before it was banned, ZAPU lost a clever young leader and organizer. He was Dr. Tichafa Parirenyatwa, the party vice-president. He was 35 years old. He was found dead in his smashed car at a railway crossing near Bulawayo. The police said it was an accident. But Africans did not believe that. His driver, who was badly injured, said they had been followed by police cars. Then they were beaten up, and the car was left at the railway crossing. He was mourned as a great loss to the nationalist movement. A line of more than 100 cars drove across the country, from Bulawayo to Murewa, for his funeral.

Government-in-Exile

Tanganyika (later Tanzania) had become independent on 9 December 1961, the same day the NDP was banned in Southern Rhodesia. In Kenya, the Mau Mau war was over and independence was near. The Federation of Rhodesia and Nyasaland was breaking up and the other two colonies were about to get independence. Northern Rhodesia would become Zambia. Nyasaland would become Malawi. Many people thought the British government was going to give independence to the

Dr. Tichafa Parirenyatwa

white minority in Southern Rhodesia, as it had done with South Africa in 1910. The African leaders did not want this. Nkomo wanted the nationalist leaders to leave the country and form a government-in-exile to oppose this. But most of the other ZAPU leaders refused. They argued that they would stay with the people, even if it meant spending many years in **detention**.

In April 1963, Nkomo finally got most of the executive to go to Tanganyika. He told them that President Nyerere had agreed to let them have a government-in-exile in his country. He told them that other African leaders also wanted this. But when they got to Dar es Salam in Tanganyika, they found Nyerere was surprised they had come. He said he knew nothing about a government-in-exile. He said the nationalist leaders should go home to Southern Rhodesia and work for majority rule.

Formation of ZANU

Some members of the ZAPU executive were unhappy with Nkomo. They thought he had been wrong to agree to the Federation and then the 1961 constitution. They thought he was not willing to fight the minority government. They thought he was spending too much time out of the country when the time had come to organize at home. And now they believed he had misled them about Nyerere's support for a government-in-exile. There were different ideas. Nkomo wanted to organize support outside the country to put pressure on the British government. Others wanted to organize the people at home to fight for independence. Nkomo would not meet some members of the executive. They began to see that they needed a new party with a new leader so they could confront the settlers.

When Nkomo heard about this, he returned to Southern Rhodesia. He **suspended** four members of the executive. These were Malianga, the secretary-general; Mugabe, the publicity secretary; Rev. Ndabaningi Sithole, the national chairman; and Takawira, the secretary for external affairs. On 8 August 1963, those four and others met at Nkala's home in Highfield. They formed a new party, the Zimbabwe African National Union (ZANU). They chose Rev. Ndabaningi Sithole as president, for the same reasons they had chosen Nkomo before. He had contacts with African leaders, and the new party would need them for political support and money to organize. Takawira became vice-president and Mugabe the secretary-general.

The new ZANU executive announced that it would work for redistribution of land, free education, the end of racial laws, control of certain industries, and so on. It was the first time an African party in Southen Rhodesia had made a public statement about the action it would take after majority rule. The ZANU leaders were confirmed at a party

Takawira, the ZAPU secretary for external affairs, and Malianga, the secretary-general were suspended. They formed ZANU, with Mugabe, Nkala and others.

Enos Nkala. ZANU was formed at his house in Highfield on 8 August 1963.

Rev. Ndabaningi Sithole was made the first president of ZANU because he had contacts with African leaders.

congress in Gweru in May 1964. A plan of action was approved. It included military action. Some of the young men at the congress had already been out of the country for military training.

Cold Comfort

Nkomo had organized a huge meeting at Cold Comfort Farm, near Harare, for 10 August 1963. The People's Caretaker Council (PCC) was formed at the farm meeting to act for the banned ZAPU party. Nkomo was made "life president of the movement". People at the meeting demanded a meeting with the British government on the future of Southern Rhodesia. They decided some leaders should prepare to leave the country and work outside. They set up committees to organize people inside the country.

Through 1963 and 1964 both parties were trying to get support among the people. Their members sometimes fought. Houses and shops were burned and looted. Many people were beaten or stabbed, and some were killed. This had occurred in other countries between nationalist parties seeking members. But it was the first time in Southern Rhodesia.

In August 1964, both ZANU and PCC were banned. The government used the excuse of inter-party fighting. But in fact many more people had been killed by the police or army, in breaking up rallies or "controlling crowds". After the banning, Mugabe, Nkomo, Sithole and hundreds of other nationalist leaders were arrested. Some were sent to prison. Others went to detention centres, such as Sikombela and Gonakudzingwa. Most of them spent the next ten years there. Many did not waste this time in detention. They spent time reading and studying. Some took time to teach other detainees.

Both parties had sent some leaders out of the country. They continued to organize support from other countries. They got young people out of the country and sent them for education or military training. They worked with friends in other countries, and with the Organization for African Unity (OAU).

The OAU was formed in May 1963. The leaders of 31 independent African countries met in Addis Ababa, the capital of Ethiopia. They wanted political and economic unity for Africa. They had many different ideas and many different kinds of government. They often did not agree. But they were united in seeking an end to colonialism, racial discrimination and *apartheid*. They set up a Liberation Committee and helped many other African countries to get independence. Moyo, Mugabe, Nkomo, Sithole and Takawira attended that first OAU meeting. They asked for money and political support. The OAU later accepted both ZANU and ZAPU. The OAU gave them money, arms and political support to fight for independence.

This picture shows Mugabe at Sikombela detention centre, where he spent his time studying and teaching other detainees. Hundreds of nationalist leaders were sent to these detention centres and some spent more than ten years there.

VOCABULARY

executive	—	leaders who decide and carry out plans.
sabotage	—	wilful damage of property during a political dispute.
restricted	—	not allowed to move out of a certain area.
government-in-exile	—	government set up outside the country to oppose the one that is inside. It has no real power unless it controls some of the land or is accepted by other governments.
detention	—	kept in a kind of prison for political reasons, without being charged in court.
suspended	—	stopped from being a party official for a time.

EXERCISES

Summary

_____ got its independence on 9 December _____. On the same day, the _____ _____ _____ was banned in _____ Rhodesia. Ten days later, the leaders formed a new party, the _____ _____ _____ _____. They worked for _____ and against _____. The vice-president was _____ _____. He was killed in August _____, a month before _____ was banned. Some executive members were unhappy with _____. They formed a new party on 8 August _____.

Questions

1. Who was General Chedu?
2. Why did most ZAPU leaders not want a government-in-exile?
3. What was approved by ZANU members at the Gweru Congress?
4. What was the Cold Comfort Farm meeting?

Discuss

Why did African leaders in Southern Rhodesia decide they would have to fight for independence?

Project

Write one letter as a group to the Department of Information, Organization of African Unity, Africa Hall, Addis Ababa, Ethiopia. Ask them to send your school some information about the OAU. Make sure that you tell them what grade you are in at school and what country you live in. Make sure you send the full postal address so their information can reach your school.

18 The Rhodesian Front and UDI

Many Europeans had moved to Southern Rhodesia after the war in Europe. They moved because they could have better jobs and a better way of life. But the growth of African nationalism made them worry. Any change in the laws about African land or labour would change the way they lived. They wanted strong action against African militants. They wanted their government to promise there would be no African rule.

Whitehead

Whitehead knew the British government would want some changes. So he gave a few more Africans the vote, more land and better jobs. He thought this African "middle class" would support his government because of these privileges. Then he took strong action against the African nationalist. His government banned the ANC in 1959, the NDP in 1961, and ZAPU in 1962.

Welensky

Roy Welensky had replaced Huggins as Prime Minister of the Federation. Huggins became Lord Malvern in 1956. Welensky was born in Southern Rhodesia. He did not like being told what to do by the British government. He wanted more independence for the Federation under white minority rule. He strongly opposed the independence of Malawi and Zambia under African governments. He argued that it was too soon, that Africans "were not ready". He called up the federal army and air force when he was arguing with the British government about this. Unlike other colonies, the Federation controlled its own defence forces.

Welensky also opposed independence for the Congo (now Zaire). He supported Tshombe's breakaway group in Katanga province. It was backed by Belgian settlers against African nationalists such as Patrice Lumumba. Lumumba is a hero of the African nationalist movements. He was a popular leader of his people. He was killed in 1961. Lumumba's death was caused by agents of a **western** capitalist government which did not like his socialist ideas. They also caused the overthrow of Nkrumah in Ghana in 1966.

Central African Break-Up

In 1963, Britain finally broke up the Federation, but not the federal armed forces. The British government gave the federal armed forces to the white minority government of Southern Rhodesia. This was agreed at the Central African Conference in 1963. The federal armed forces were very powerful. There were many planes in the air force. African leaders were angry with the British government for giving this power to the minority

Edgar Whitehead was prime minister after Todd. He banned the ANC, NDP and ZAPU.

Roy Welensky was prime minister of the Federation after Huggins. He opposed independence for Malawi, Zaire and Zambia.

Patrice Lumumba was Prime Minister of the Congo (Zaire), an African hero killed for his socialist ideas.

government. Nkrumah told Britain that he thought the white minority would use the air force to kill African people in Southern Africa. This proved to be true.

Rise of the Rhodesian Front

Late in 1962 the settlers had elected a new government. It did not want to work with Africans. The leaders promised to take any action to protect white **supremacy**. This was the Rhodesian Front. It was formed in March 1962. The Rhodesian Reform Party led by John Gaunt and Ian Smith joined with the Dominion Party led by Winston Field. Field became leader of the new RF party.

The RF did not want majority rule. But they did not want British colonial rule either. They wanted independence to be given to the white minority government. Some members of the RF began to worry that Field would not push for independence if Britain refused to give it to the white minority. So they changed their leader. They removed Field in April 1964. The new leader of the RF was Ian Smith. He became the Prime Minister of Southern Rhodesia.

Winston Field was the first leader of the Rhodesian Front. RF members thought he would not push Britain over independence for white Rhodesia.

Ian Smith

Smith was a farmer. He had been a pilot of fighter planes in the British air force during the war in Europe. He was born in Southern Rhodesia.

Smith argued with the British government about independence for 18 months. While he was arguing he was also preparing. He was getting ready to make an illegal **declaration** of independence, if Britain would not agree to it on his terms. He detained African nationalist leaders. His government took over the radio and television so that only the views of the RF could be heard. He banned newspapers, such as the African Daily News, that wrote about African grievances. Books about protest movements and nationalist leaders in other African countries were also banned. The army commander did not agree with what Smith was doing. So Smith dismissed him. He named a new army commander who agreed with what he was doing

Then Smith called a meeting of 622 chiefs and headmen. He asked them to accept independence under the 1961 constitution. The chiefs were paid by Smith's government. So if they voted against illegal independence they could be replaced. Smith said the chiefs and headmen spoke for all Africans in Southern Rhodesia. He said Africans had agreed to the 1961 constitution. But this was not true. Then he held a referendum for all white adults. There were 58 000 votes for independence under a white minority government and 6 000 votes against.

Ian Smith soon took over as RF leader. He spent the next 18 months preparing for illegal independence.

UDI

Smith called a general election in May 1965. The RF won all 50 seats in parliament. White Rhodesians wanted independence. But they did not want majority rule. They had elected a government that promised to protect white privileges for all time. Smith said: "If in my lifetime we have an African nationalist government in Southern Rhodesia, then we will have failed in the policy that I believe in."

On 11 November 1965, Smith made his **Unilateral** Declaration of Independence (UDI). He said a government of Rhodesia would be set up under the 1961 constitution. He knew that Britain would not take action to stop him. He controlled the federal defence forces. Britain would not send its army to fight against them. Smith knew this, and so did everyone else, because the British Prime Minister, Harold Wilson, said so several times. Many people thought this was a way of telling Smith to go ahead. So Smith was in a strong position. He held all the white seats in parliament. He knew that the British government woud not send an army to stop him. And he knew that many businessmen would continue to trade with his illegal government.

Smith signed the Unilateral Declaration of Independence (UDI) on 11 November 1965 and set the course for 15 years of white minority rule. Then the nationalists knew for certain that they would have to fight.

Harold Wilson was the British Prime Minister at the time. He refused to send British soldiers against the settlers.

Joanna V, one of the ships that broke sanctions and carried oil to Rhodesia.

United Nations

The United Nations is a place where people from most countries in the world meet to talk about their problems and try to solve them. The UN was formed in 1945, after the last big war in Europe. Representatives from almost all independent countries meet in the UN General Assembly. The underdeveloped countries of Africa, Asia and South America now form the majority in the General Assembly. But any action suggested by the General Assembly must be agreed to by a smaller group called the Security Council. Britain, China, France, the Soviet Union, and the United States are the five permanent members of the Security Council. Other members are chosen every two years. The five permanent members can each say "no" to any action. That is called a **veto**. When African countries asked Britain to use military force to stop the rebellion in Rhodesia, Britain used its veto in the Security Council. It said "no".

Sanctions

Nine African countries broke relations with Britain because it did not take action against UDI. The UN voted to stop all trade with the illegal government. This is called **sanctions**. The UN hoped that this would force the Rhodesian Front to change their mind. But the white rebels of Rhodesia ruled for 15 years.

One reason why UDI lasted so long was that businessmen from many countries continued to trade with Rhodesia. They broke the UN sanctions. Oil companies supplied fuel through South Africa to Rhodesia. One of these oil companies was partly owned by the British government. The white minority government used this petrol to keep its industry going, and to keep the army and air force fighting. The United States government broke the UN sanctions for some time. It allowed its companies to buy Rhodesian chrome metal. South Africa traded freely with Rhodesia throughout UDI. Many companies in other countries bought and sold things to Rhodesia through South Africa. South Africa later supplied Rhodesia with a lot of weapons and spare parts.

The settlers learned to look after things and make them last a long time. They learned to make many things themselves instead of importing them. They learned to depend on themselves. This is one lesson we can learn from this period — self-reliance.

Nkrumah warned that the Federal air force would be used against Africans.

VOCABULARY

western	—	often used to mean the capitalist countries of Western Europe and the Americas, led by the United States. Eastern is often used to mean the socialist countries of Eastern Europe and Asia, led by the Soviet Union and China.
supremacy	—	being the highest or most important.
declaration	—	statement.
unilateral	—	without consulting others.
veto	—	to reject something or say no.
sanctions	—	pressures to obey a law. Economic sanctions were imposed on Rhodesia to stop trade with other countries and try to force the white minority to negotiate.

EXERCISES

Summary

_____ was leader of the government that banned the _____ in 1959, _____ in 1961, and _____ in 1962. The Prime Minister of the Federation was _____. He wanted more independence for the _____. But he was opposed to independence for _____ and _____. He also opposed independence for the _____. A popular leader of the people there was _____. He was killed in _____. _____ warned Britain that the white minority would use the federal defence forces against African people in _____ _____.

Questions
1. What did Smith do to prepare for UDI?
2. How did Smith and everyone else know that the British government would not try to stop UDI?
3. Why did the Rhodesian Front declare UDI?
4. Why did the UN agree that no one should trade with Rhodesia?
5. Why and how did some companies continue to trade with Rhodesia?

Discuss
Self-reliance. The settlers were forced to be self-reliant because of sanctions. They were strong because they were self-reliant. They made many things they needed instead of getting them from outside the country. What lesson can we learn from this today?

Project

Make up a play about the UN General Assembly. Every student can act as the representative of a different country, big or small. There are many more countries than there are students in your class, even if it is a very big class. The teacher or a student can be the chairman. He or she controls the meeting and says who will speak next. This "General Assembly" can discuss the idea of imposing sanctions against Rhodesia. In this case Zimbabwe would not be present because it was not yet independent. Or the "General Assembly" can discuss some other issue such as the independence of Namibia. Then Zimbabwe would be a member of the General Assembly and could speak about the problem. Or you could find a story in the newspaper about something that happened at the UN, and discuss that. This way you can learn about the UN, and you can also learn how to run a meeting.

UNITED NATIONS
New York, 1980
Almost every country in the world, big or small, is a member of the UN.

19 The Armed Struggle

The nationalist movement grew. So did its demands. We have already seen that Africans were no longer demanding only better pay and working conditions, and equal rights. They now wanted majority rule. The 1961 constitution was too late in offering 15 African seats in parliament. By then it had to be equal seats with Europeans. Some NDP leaders saw that they would have to fight for equality and independence. After the banning of ZAPU in September 1962, there was more pressure from the youth for militant action. A few more young men were sent out of the country for military training. Others stayed in the country to throw petrol bombs and hand grenades. The protests grew more violent. Toward the end of 1963 and early 1964, bombs were placed on railway lines, electricity stations, and sometimes private homes.

The Early Days

Early in 1964, trained **guerrillas** from both ZANU and ZAPU were **infiltrated** into Rhodesia. One ZAPU group was caught crossing the Victoria Falls Bridge from Zambia with explosives in the back of their car. A ZANU group, led by Emmerson Mnangagwa, walked across the bridge at Chirundu. They looked young so the border officials thought they were school boys. They did not carry any guns or explosives. They got their weapons inside the country. Mnangagwa's group got their first rifles from Rhodesian soldiers, who had left them piled in a corner at a dance at Domboshawa. People working in the mines sometimes took explosives and gave them to the guerrillas. Mnangagwa and others from his group attended the Gweru congress of ZANU in 1964. But few people knew they were trained guerrillas.

Young men who were out of the country for training when the parties split had to choose whether to stay with ZAPU or join ZANU. Eleven out of 13 young men who were training in Egypt joined ZANU. Five of them, led by Mnangagwa, went to China for training in September. This early training lasted for six months. They learned how to use weapons, and how to blow up economic targets such as bridges and railway lines.

Emmerson Mnangagwa, one of the first trained guerrillas to infiltrate Rhodesia.

The Crocodile Gang

One group which took militant action that year had no weapons and no training. This was the Crocodile Gang. On 4 July 1964, they stopped a car near Chimanimani and killed the driver with a knife. The driver was a Rhodesian Front chairman in the area. He was the first white person killed in a nationalist uprising since the 1890s. The Crocodile Gang showed that with courage it was possible to fight, even without guns.

Many nationalist leaders, and many of the young guerrillas, were arrested in August 1964 and detained. But both ZANU and ZAPU had sent some leaders out of the country. The ZANU national chairman, Herbert Chitepo, was in Tanzania where he was a senior legal adviser to that government. He was the first African lawyer in Southern Rhodesia. ZAPU had decided to send Moyo, Edward Ndlovu, and Silundika to Zambia.

Battle of Chinhoyi

When UDI was declared in 1965 the nationalist leaders knew their battle would be long. More young men went for training and were infiltrated into the country. The first battle of the war took place near Chinhoyi on 28 April 1966. Seven ZANU guerrillas were killed in a fierce battle with the Rhodesian police. The police brought in helicopters and soldiers. The fighting lasted several hours. The seven were part of a group of 21 guerrillas. Later, some attacked a farm at Chegutu and others headed for the Charter area. ZANU remembers the Battle of Chinhoyi as Chimurenga Day, the start of the liberation war.

Hwange Battles

In July 1967, a large force of ZAPU guerrillas were infiltrated across the Zambezi River into Hwange Game Reserve. Some members of the African National Congress (ANC) of South Africa were with them. They hoped that they would bring the day of independence for their own country closer by helping to liberate Zimbabwe. Through August and September there were a series of battles between the guerrillas and the Rhodesian Army. Seven Rhodesian soldiers were killed and fourteen wounded. These were the first Rhodesian military **casualties** of the war. The South African government sent **paramilitary** police to help the Rhodesians. They thought they could protect their own country by protecting Rhodesia. Most of the guerrillas were killed or captured.

Difficulties

The next year there were more battles. Many ZAPU guerrillas were killed, wounded or captured. The Rhodesians used the old federal defence forces which they were given by Britain. They had bigger guns. They had armoured cars. They had fighter planes, bombers and armed helicopters. The guerrillas were not able to defend themselves against attacks from the air. The people in the villages had not been told what was happening and what to expect. They did not know what the war was about. They were afraid of the guns. Some people talked about fighting, but very few then were prepared to die for independence.

It was not easy to send guerrillas across the Zambezi River. People crossing the river could easily be seen. For those who were able to cross safely there were other problems. There was little water to drink. There were few people living near the river to give food and shelter.

Herbert Chitepo, the ZANU national chairman, went to Zambia from Tanzania in 1966 as external leader of the armed struggle.

Jason Moyo, the second vice-president of ZAPU was sent to Zambia in 1964 to continue the struggle.

By the end of 1968 the nationalist leaders knew they had to find a new **approach** to the struggle. Many people had been killed. Others had gone to prison. Some were hanged in prison. They were losing too many people, and they were not any closer to majority rule. For the next four years there was very little fighting, while the guerrilla leaders worked out a new approach.

Other Struggles

Some other colonies in Southern Africa had also decided to fight for independence. The Popular Movement for the Liberation of Angola (MPLA) had begun fighting against the Portuguese in Angola in 1961. The Front for the Liberation of Mozambique (FRELIMO) began to fight against the Portuguese in their country in 1964. The South West Africa People's Organization (SWAPO) began to fight against the South Africans in Namibia in 1966.

Nyerere and Tanzania

President Nyerere and the government of Tanzania helped all of these struggles before other countries were independent. The Tanzanian people were very poor, but they gave what little they had to share with the other people still fighting for freedom in Africa. This was a **principle** that both Nkrumah and Nyerere believed — that no African country is free until all of Africa is free. The Tanzanian people gave food and shelter. Their radio gave air time for broadcasts by nationalist movements in neighbouring countries. Tanzania hosted the OAU Liberation Committee, and gave military training to many liberation armies.

The military training was not easy. The day began at 4.30 in the morning with exercises. Then the trainees ran for 16 miles. After the first four months, they ran carrying full equipment. Political education started at 7.00 in the morning. And then there was military training — how to use a gun and look after it, how to use landmines and explosives. The recruits learned about the national grievances. That is the problems faced by the people at home over land, labour, education, health and so on. They learned their history. And they prepared to go home and fight for independence and majority rule.

Tanzania was one of the first countries in the region to get its independence, in 1961. Then the Tanzanian people shared what little resources they had to help other people in other countries to get their independence.

VOCABULARY

guerrillas	—	freedom fighters, later called "the boys" and "the girls".
infiltrated	—	crossed into without attracting attention.
casualties	—	people killed or wounded.
paramilitary	—	part time military, with some military training but not full time soldiers.
approach	—	way of doing things.
principle	—	moral truth or guiding rule that a person lives by.

EXERCISES

Summary

The _____ Gang struck in July _____. Soon after that, many _____ leaders were detained. But both _____ and _____ had some leaders out of the country. The Battle of _____ was on 28 April _____. Seven _____ guerrillas were killed. This is also called _____ Day. In July _____ a large force of _____ guerrillas crossed the _____ River and entered the _____ Game Reserve. They had many battles with _____ soldiers. Some members of the _____ of South Africa were with them. Soon after this the _____ _____ government sent paramilitary _____ to _____. They thought they would protect their country by protecting _____. Most of the guerrillas were killed or _____.

Questions
1. Who was Herbert Chitepo?
2. Why did the guerrillas suffer heavy losses in the 1960s?
3. What did President Nyerere and the people of Tanzania do to help so many other countries to be free?

Discuss

Living together. Why is no African country free until all of Africa is free? What is the meaning of this principle shared by Nkrumah and Nyerere? How did other African countries help Zimbabwe to become independent? What is the OAU Liberation Committee that you also read about in an earlier chapter?

Project

Find someone who received military training or education in another country. Ask them about why they went and what they learned. Learn something about the country they were in. Write down the story and bring it to school. Some stories could be read to other students and discussed.

Armed Struggle Begins: The First Attacks, 1966-68

1. Battle of Chinhoyi (ZANU) 28 April 1966
2. Hwange Battle (ZAPU) July-September 1967
3. Tete Offensive (FRELIMO) begins 7-8 March 1968

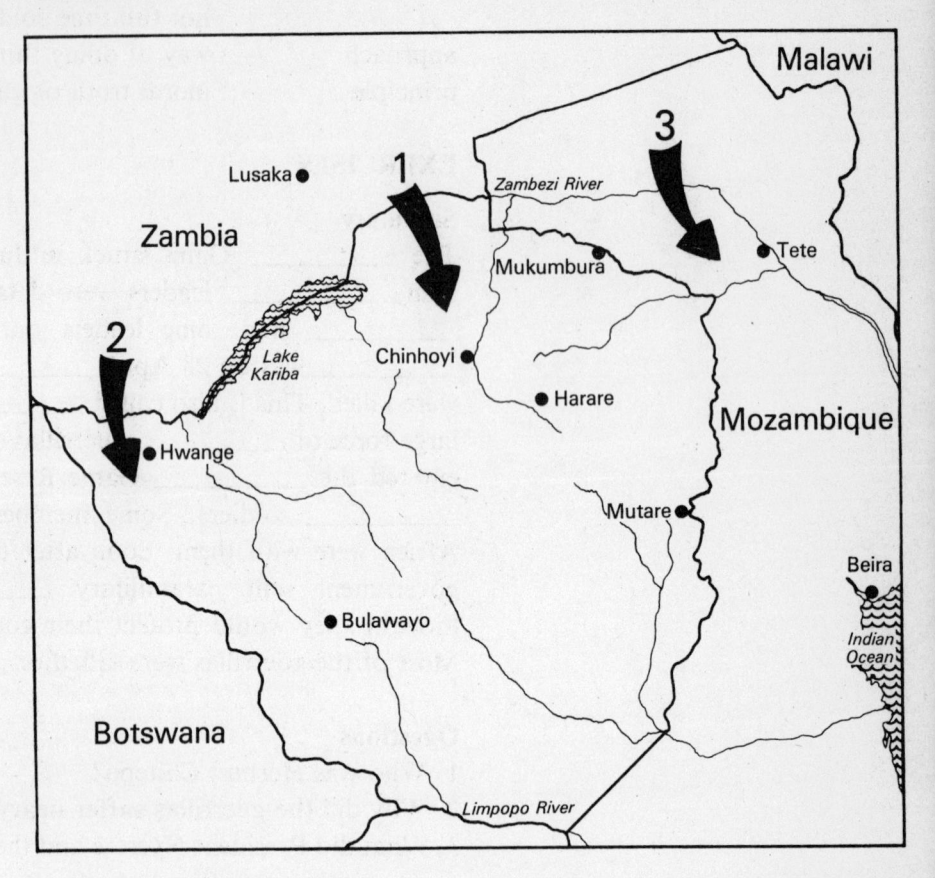

20 The Pearce Commission and the new ANC

Britain was still the colonial power over Rhodesia. British companies wanted to do business with Rhodesia. But they wanted some changes. They did not want an **unstable** country near South Africa because many of them had investments there. So the British government tried to talk to Smith about legal independence. Smith would not go to Britain. He could be arrested there for **treason** because of UDI. So the British Prime Minister, Harold Wilson, met him twice on British warships.

"Tiger"

Wilson met Smith on the warship "Tiger" in 1966. The plan Wilson suggested did not include majority rule. He said Rhodesia was not ready for majority rule. The proposals offered more African seats in the senate and gave more power to the chiefs. There would be a **transition** of four months before the constitution became law. Britain promised to use military force if the new law was broken by anyone. The Rhodesian Front did not accept these proposals.

"Fearless"

Smith and Wilson met again in 1968 on the warship "Fearless". The proposals were almost the same. But there was no transition and no promise to send British armed forces to keep the law. The British government had given in on some major points. And there was still no promise of majority rule. African leaders were very angry with the British government. They told Britain to withdraw the proposals. Many members of Wilson's own Labour Party government did not agree with what he suggested. His plan was to give legal independence to the racist government. But the RF refused again.

These talks were always held late in the year when the rains were starting. The rain made it easier for the freedom fighters to move around. Water was easier to find. The leaves on the trees and the long grass gave better cover. The muddy roads made it difficult for the Rhodesian army trucks to move. The African nationalists knew that Smith had to be forced to talk. He always agreed to talk after some guerrilla action. The "Tiger" talks came after the Battle of Chinoyi. The "Fearless" talks followed the Hwange battles.

Republic

The UN economic sanctions proved to have more effect over a long time than a short time. After some years, the sanctions on exports caused a shortage of money to buy imported goods. This meant there were fewer spare parts for machines. Rhodesian industry began to have trouble. So did the transport system. But in 1968 sanctions had not yet had this ef-

Smith and Wilson met twice on British warships, but they could not agree. African leaders were very angry with Wilson because he did not push for majority rule.

fect. The RF was strong. It was moving further away from any settlement that could be accepted by Africans.

In May 1969 the RF made up its own racist constitution. There would be 66 members of parliament. Fifty seats would be elected by whites. Only eight seats would be elected by Africans. Eight other members would be chosen by the chiefs, headmen and local councils. The number of African members could change after some time. But this depended on the total amount of income tax paid by Africans. African salaries were very low. So the total amount of income tax was also low. It would take a very long time to increase the number of African members in parliament. This constitution said there could never be more than 50 African seats. This was the same number as white seats. The African majority would never be allowed to control the government.

The whites voted in favour of this. On 2 March 1970, Rhodesia declared itself a **republic**. Ian Smith was still the Prime Minister and Clifford Dupont was the President. Ten days later there was another election. The RF again won all 50 white seats in parliament. A few months later, the government in Britain changed. The Conservative Party came to power, led by Edward Heath. The new government sent **envoys** to talk to the Rhodesian Front. After several months, Smith signed an agreement with the British Foreign Secretary, Sir Alex Douglas-Home. They did not agree to majority rule. They agreed to continue minority rule. So Africans leaders were very angry with the Conservative government in Britain. So were some members of the Labour Party in Britain.

Sir Alex Douglas-Home, the British Foreign Secretary, signed an agreement with Smith in 1971, but it was not majority rule.

NIBMAR

In 1965 the British government had agreed to five principles. These principles had to be met before legal independence could be given to Rhodesia. The principles were: (1) moves towards majority rule, (2) no changes to the constitution that did not move in this way, (3) more political rights for Africans, (4) moves to end racial discrimination, (5) any agreement must be approved by all Rhodesians, black and white. The nationalists used this last principle as a political **slogan**. They called it NIBMAR. That meant "No Independence Before Majority Rule".

Smith argued that the chiefs and headmen were able to speak for the majority. But the British knew the chiefs were paid by Smith's government and were not free to oppose white rule. So the British government set up a commission to find out what Africans thought about the new agreement. The commission was headed by Lord Pearce. So it was called the Pearce Commission. Smith thought Africans would accept the agreement. The British government and British companies also thought the answer would be 'yes'. But the people said 'no' because they wanted real majority rule.

Lord Pearce headed a commission to find out what Africans thought of the agreement.

The African National Council

Most nationalist leaders were still in detention. Their parties were banned. So the people needed a new nationalist party to tell the commission that they did not want this agreement. Members of ZANU and ZAPU formed a joint committee. The four people on the committee were Edson Sithole and Eddison Zvobgo from ZANU, Josiah Chinamano and Cephas Msipa from ZAPU. They agreed to form a new party called the African National Council (ANC) to oppose the agreement.

The first man offered the job of leading the new movement was Chief Rekayi Tangwena. He was a respected nationalist. He was not like most of the other chiefs. He was trying to stop the RF government from forcing his people to move off their land. So he was too busy to take on another job. The second choice was Bishop Abel Muzorewa. He was head of the United Methodist Church. He had been speaking out against the racist government. The ANC was formed on 16 December 1971. ZANU and ZAPU had an equal number of members in the leadership. When a secretary was from one party, the deputy came from another party.

ZANU and ZAPU were banned but the members formed a new party to oppose the agreement. They called it the African National Council (ANC) and asked Chief Rekayi Tangwena to lead it.

"No"

The ANC was formed only four weeks before the Pearce Commission was to begin. So the nationalists had to work fast. They could not use the radio, television and newspapers because these were controlled by the RF. Smith thought the chiefs and headmen would get Africans to agree to the new plan. The RF spent a lot of money to make sure the answer was 'yes'. The ANC had very little money. The RF refused to allow the ANC to hold meetings to oppose the settlement. The British Government agreed with this because they thought the plan should be accepted. The ANC worked very hard organizing the people. It was the first time since the coming of the settlers that the African majority had been asked what it wanted. Smith said the ANC was forcing people to reject the proposals. But this was not true. The people did not want this agreement. They wanted majority rule. They did not trust the RF to make an agreement that would help them.

On 4 May 1972, Lord Pearce gave the report of his commission. He said the proposals were not accepted by the majority of Africans in Rhodesia. The people had said "No". This was the first national resistance by Africans against the settlers since 1896.

Bishop Abel Muzorewa became the leader of the ANC because Tangwena was busy trying to save the land for his people.

VOCABULARY

unstable	—	not steady, likely to change.
treason	—	acting against your own country.
transition	—	a period of time allowed to change from one way of government to another.
republic	—	state headed by an elected leader, not by a king or queen.
envoys	—	officials sent on a special job by their government.
slogan	—	word or words used to organize people.

EXERCISES

Summary

The British Prime Minister, _____ _____, met Smith twice on British warships. They were called _____ and _____. The plan he suggested did not include _____ _____. The plan was to give legal independence to the _____ government. In _____ the RF made up its own constitution. This allowed for _____ seats in parliament. _____ seats could be elected by whites. _____ seats would be elected by Africans. _____ seats would be chosen by _____, headmen and national councils. Rhodesia declared itself a _____ in 1970. A few days later, there was an election and the RF won all _____ white seats.

Questions

1. Why was it easier for the freedom fighters after the rains began?
2. What was the Pearce Commission?
3. Who formed the ANC?
4. What is the meaning of NIBMAR?

Discuss

Communication. The majority of Africans in Rhodesia were against the constitution proposals in 1971. Why was this not reported by the radio, television and press? Why were the nationalists not allowed to address meetings?

Project

Rain is very important in our daily lives. It helped the guerrillas during the war. It helps the trees to grow. It helps the grass to grow for the cattle to eat. It helps our crops to grow tall and full. When the rain does not come we can suffer and even go hungry. Write a story about the rain, and what it means to your family, and what we can do when it does not come.

21 A New Approach to the Struggle

Many friendly countries gave military training to members of ZANU and ZAPU in the 1960s and 1970s. Some of these were Algeria, Cuba, Egypt, Ghana, Rumania, the Soviet Union, Tanzania and Yugoslavia. Western socialist countries such as Denmark and Sweden gave clothes, blankets, books and medicine. Some UN committees helped. So did the OAU, as we have seen. Most western capitalist governments did not help. But some people in those countries helped, even when their governments did not. They formed solidarity groups to raise money and distribute information.

Training was not easy. There was physical and political training as well as learning how to use a gun.

China

The two countries which helped the most in finding a new approach to the struggle were China and Mozambique. They had good ideas about how to **mobilize** the people for a **protracted** struggle. The third ZANU group that went to China for military training in 1966 was led by Josiah Tongogara. He became ZANU's Secretary for Defence and the most important guerrilla leader of the war.

Tongogara went to live in Zambia in 1960 because he could not get any more education at home. He met Mnangagwa's guerrilla group in 1964. They had just returned from China. He heard about their training and what they had learned. He soon left his job and went for military training. First he went to Itumbi in south-western Tanzania. That was the first permanent training camp for the ZANU Liberation Army, ZANLA. Then Tongogara went to China. The ideas he learned about **mass** mobilization were very important in forming ZANU's new approach.

Josiah Tongogara, the ZANLA commander, trained in Tanzania and then China in 1966. This picture of him with Josiah Tungamirai, the ZANLA Political Commissar, was taken during the war.

Mao Tse Tung wrote about three stages of guerrilla war. The first stage is to mobilize the people so they can understand what the war is about. There is little fighting at this time. Roads are mined. There are some ambushes and sabotage. When the people have been mobilized, the guerrillas can easily get food, shelter and information. Then the second stage begins. The guerrillas attack the enemy in larger numbers. They take more and more of the countryside away from the enemy. They train the people to defend themselves. They help the people to set up schools, clinics and a new administration. The people are free to plough and plant their crops again. Then comes the third and final stage when the towns are surrounded and attacked, and the existing government gives way to the freedom fighters.

Mozambique

Some members of the ZANLA High Command during the war.

In March 1968, Frelimo opened a new area of operations in Tete province, bordering on the north-east of Rhodesia. By early 1971, Frelimo was fighting south of the Zambezi River and all the way to the Rhodesian

107

border near Mukumbura. This meant that Frelimo guerrillas could help Zimbabwean fighters to infiltrate into Rhodesia. This new way was not as difficult as crossing the Zambezi River from Zambia.

The Rhodesian army often went into Tete to help the Portuguese army fight against Frelimo. The leaders of Frelimo knew that this would continue unless the Rhodesians were kept busy at home. They knew Mozambique could not be free unless the people of Zimbabwe were also freed from colonial rule. So they wanted to help the Zimbabweans to fight.

At that time, the Frelimo leaders were more friendly with ZAPU. Both Frelimo and ZAPU got most of their money and weapons from the Soviet Union. So Frelimo asked ZAPU if they wanted to send fighters into Rhodesia through Tete. But the offer came at a very bad time for ZAPU. There was a leadership **crisis** and the leaders were divided. Nkomo was still in prison in Rhodesia. Two main ZAPU leaders outside Rhodesia had broken away from the party. These were Chikerema and Nyandoro. They joined some ZANU members in forming a new party called the Front for the Liberation of Zimbabwe (Frolizi). This party did not last very long. But it caused a lot of trouble for the other ZAPU leaders, such as Moyo and Silundika. They were even detained for a time in Zambia. So when Frelimo asked them to send fighters, they were unable to do so.

Training with Frelimo

At the same time, the *Dare reChimurenga* (war council) of ZANU was asking Frelimo to allow ZANLA to infiltrate through Mozambique. The *Dare* hoped that ZANU guerrillas could use the new route to begin their new approach. They wanted to mobilize the people before beginning to fight. The military leaders of Frelimo and ZANU met twice in Lusaka, in November 1969 and May 1970. At the second meeting, they agreed to work together.

In July 1970, ZANU sent the first four guerrillas to join Frelimo in Tete. They had learned the theory of guerrilla war at Itumbi. Now they were going to put this into practice. They learned how to hide weapons so they could be found and used later. They learned how to keep prisoners, and what to do if a comrade fell sick on a march. They learned how to cross a river before drinking to make sure there were no enemy forces on the other side. They learned how to live with the people in the rural areas. They saw Frelimo teaching people how to improve their lives by using **co-operative** agriculture.

This was a difficult time in Tete. The guerrillas were often bombed by airplanes. Sometimes they had to eat roots, wild honey, berries, bugs and wild animals. But Frelimo was taking control of more land, and the way into Rhodesia was getting safer. On 4 December 1971, the first two guerrillas crossed into north-eastern Rhodesia from Tete. Their job was to meet people and begin to mobilize them for war.

Recruiting

ZANLA guerrillas **recruited** many people in the north-east during the next year. One group of old men travelled to Mozambique to ask for weapons and guerrillas to start fighting. The old men collected the passes, called *situpas*, from young men who went out for training. These were given to trained men going into Rhodesia. They could show these if they were stopped by the police or army, and no one would know that they were freedom fighters.

The guerrillas organized the spirit mediums. One important recruit was Mbuya Nehanda. Many people believed she was the medium for the same spirit who inspired people to join the First *Chimurenga* in 1896. Mbuya Nehanda was a small, old woman. The guerrillas carried her to their main rear base in Mozambique. This was at Chifombo, near the border with Zambia. She stayed at the camp and often gave advice to ZANLA guerrillas on their way into Rhodesia. Inside the country, other mediums helped to mobilize the people for a new kind of struggle.

Several women were among the new recruits. They told the men that women were also oppressed and wanted to fight to free themselves. During the next two years, many women carried weapons into the country. They walked from Chifombo carrying loads of guns and bullets on their backs. Each trip took many weeks. They carried buckets of mealie meal on their heads to eat on the way. Late in 1972, the people and the weapons were ready. A group of 60 ZANLA guerrillas were infiltrated.

The Decisive Phase

The **decisive phase** of the war had begun. The first attack took place on 21 December 1972. This was at Altena Farm in the Centenary area. It was owned by a white farmer who treated his workers badly. In the next two weeks, ten Rhodesian soldiers were wounded, and one killed while they were looking for the guerrillas. They did not find them. The guerrillas got help from Chief Chiweshe, and had their first base in his area.

When the guerrillas opened a new area they had to learn about the place and the people. They had to learn where to camp and where to hide their weapons, which paths to use and where to get water. They had to learn the people's grievances. These were mostly about land and education. They had to know who they could trust for information, food and shelter, and who were the sell-outs who would tell the enemy of their presence. They often talked to farm workers about how they were treated, and asked if there was a Rhodesian army base on the farm.

The spirit mediums played an important part in mobilizing the people for the struggle, just as they had done in the First Chimurenga Chipfeni and Chidyamauyu were two mediums active in the north-east.

Teurai Ropa was one of the first women to train inside the country. She later became ZANU Secretary for Women's Affairs.

The Decisive Phase of the War Begins, 1972

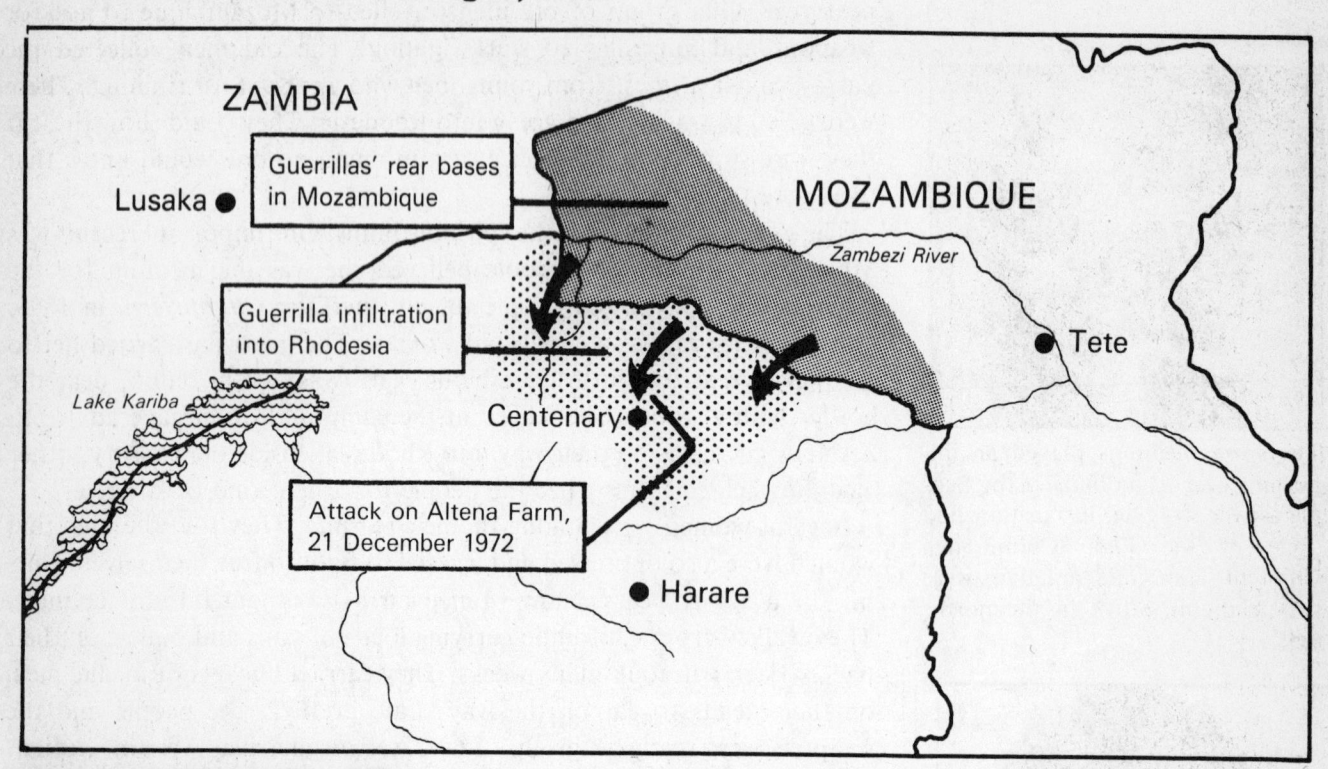

Map showing Zambia, Mozambique, and Rhodesia with labels: Lusaka, Guerrillas' rear bases in Mozambique, Guerrilla infiltration into Rhodesia, Lake Kariba, Centenary, Attack on Altena Farm, 21 December 1972, Harare, Zambezi River, Tete.

The kalashnikov gun became a symbol of freedom, but political education went with military training. There was a code of conduct that taught the young guerrillas how to use the gun to defend and liberate the people.

The war spread quickly through the north-east. The guerrillas went to the farming areas around Centenary, Dande, Chesa and Mount Darwin. They organized people to support the struggle to liberate themselves. They attacked police posts and blew up small bridges. They captured a young white man called Gerald Hawksworth and held him for a year before releasing him unharmed. By March 1973 there had been more than 200 attacks. But the RF government announced less than 40 attacks. They did not want Rhodesians to know how serious it was. These attacks had surprised the government. It was a new way of fighting. The guerrillas did not fight big battles. They made small attacks and then disappeared among the people. The war in the north-east began to hurt the Rhodesian economy. It was costing a lot of money to chase the guerrillas. The army and air force were using more petrol. The government soon had to limit the amount of petrol other people could use.

Zambia

At first Smith thought the guerrillas were coming from Zambia as they had done in the past. So he closed the border with Zambia soon after the attack on Altena Farm. Then he found that they were coming through Mozambique. So he wanted to open the border again. He said the Zambian government had promised to stop guerrillas from crossing the Zambezi River. But President Kaunda said he had not promised this, and he kept the border closed until 1978.

Zambia is landlocked like Zimbabwe. That means that any trade going from Zambia to the sea must pass through other countries. There was fighting in Angola to the west of Zambia. There was fighting in Mozambique, to the east. So most of Zambia's trade went south, through Rhodesia. Then that border was closed. A new trade route to the sea was built from Zambia to Dar es Salaam in Tanzania. But it was still costing Zambia a lot of money to get exports out and imports in. Through 1973 and 1974, the freedom fighters in Angola, Mozambique, Namibia and Rhodesia were spreading the liberation struggle. Zambian leaders began to talk to the leaders of Portugal and South Africa to try to stop the war.

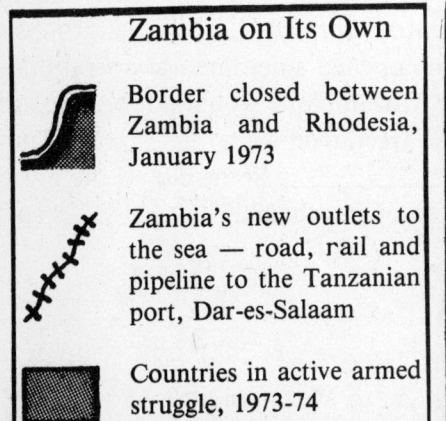

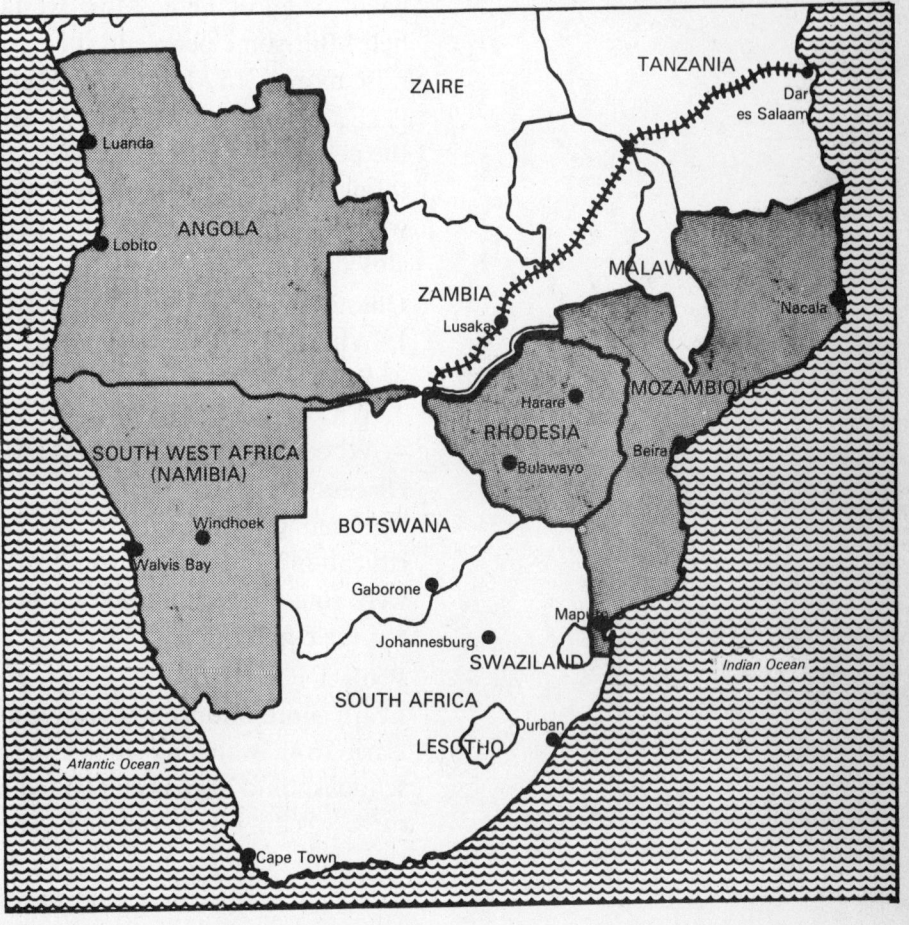

Zambia on Its Own

- Border closed between Zambia and Rhodesia, January 1973
- Zambia's new outlets to the sea — road, rail and pipeline to the Tanzanian port, Dar-es-Salaam
- Countries in active armed struggle, 1973-74

VOCABULARY

mobilize	— bring people together in support of something.
protracted	— taking a long time.
mass	— of the people.
crisis	— a serious problem.
co-operative	— working together with other people to produce something for the good of all.
recruited	— got people to join.
decisive phase	— the time which decides how things will go. This was the beginning of the end of white rule in Rhodesia.

EXERCISES

Summary

Many friendly countries gave military training. Some of these were _____, _____ and _____. _____ governments gave the most help. Most western _____ governments did not help. But some people in their countries formed _____ groups to raise money. In March 1968 Frelimo opened a new area of operations in _____ province. They knew Mozambique would not be free until the people of _____ were also freed from _____ rule. Smith thought the guerrillas came from _____. So he closed the border with _____. When he tried to open it again, _____ kept it closed.

Questions

1. Who was Josiah Tongogara?
2. What was Mao's theory of guerrilla war?
3. Why could ZAPU not send fighters to Mozambique?
4. Who was Mbuya Nehanda?

Discuss

National grievances. Why were the main grievances about land and education? From what you have read in this and earlier chapters, what were some of the other grievances? Why did the people decide to fight for their rights?

Project

Learn more about co-operative agriculture and how it works. You can learn from watching yourselves. The crops you have planted at your school should have been planted by all of you. Students should be taking turns weeding and watering. Then when the vegetables are ready, you share this among yourselves. Or you sell the products and the money goes to some school project. So you will all benefit. This is a co-operative. You can learn more about co-operatives by asking someone from the district council or the Ministry of Agriculture to come to your school and talk about this.

22 The Portuguese Coup D'Etat and Detente

On 25 April 1974, there was a **coup d'état** in Portugal. This changed the history of Southern Africa. The Portuguese army had been fighting against nationalist guerrillas in Africa for 13 years. This was in Angola, Guinea-Bissau and Mozambique. More than 7 000 Portuguese soldiers had died in these wars. Many thousands more were wounded. Many Portuguese **officers** knew they could not defeat the guerrillas. But their government refused to give independence to the African colonies. So in 1974 the officers removed their government in a *coup d'état*. This was called the Movement of the Armed Forces (MFA). They became the new government of Portugal. The people in Portugal were very happy. They had been oppressed for many years under the **dictators** Salazar and Caetano. Now they were free. They gave flowers to the soldiers to thank them for bringing peace and freedom.

Portuguese Colonies Free

The officers did not want to continue fighting in the colonies. But they were not sure what to do next. So the guerrillas of Frelimo, MPLA and PAIGC kept on fighting. They won more battles. After a few weeks, the new Portuguese government agreed to majority rule. This ended 500 years of Portuguese colonial rule. The PAIGC had already declared that Guinea-Bissau was independent on 24 September 1973. But the Portuguese government did not accept this until after the *coup d'état*. The Portuguese army withdrew from the colonies. Mozambique became independent on 25 June 1975, and Angola on 11 November 1975.

The independence of Angola and Mozambique was very important for their neighbours, Namibia and Rhodesia. SWAPO guerrillas now had a friendly country on the border with Namibia. They moved most of their people to Angola. The independence of Mozambique meant that Zimbabwean guerrillas could operate along the entire border of more than 1 000 kilometres, instead of only through the province of Tete.

Detente

The governments and armies of Portugal, Rhodesia and South Africa had worked together to prevent majority rule in Southern Rhodesia. They fought together against the guerrillas. Then Angola and Mozambique became independent. Their governments supported the nationalists. They did not support the racist governments of Rhodesia and South Africa. So the white minority governments began to look for ways to stop the nationalists coming to power in Namibia and Rhodesia.

The Zambian government had been secretly talking with the Portuguese government before the *coup d'état*. Now Zambia began to talk with South Africa. This talking to the enemy is called **detente**.

President Kaunda of Zambia had talks with the Portuguese and the South Africans in an exercise called detente.

Herbert Chitepo, the ZANU national chairman, was killed in Zambia by Rhodesian agents who wanted to destroy the party and stop the war.

Lusaka Agreement

The leaders of the **frontline** African countries invited some Zimbabwean leaders to meet in Lusaka. The frontline leaders wanted them to unite. They thought this would make them stronger if they had to negotiate with Smith about majority rule. They thought if the leaders were not united then Smith might be able to make a separate deal with one of them. Sithole was invited as ZANU leader, Nkomo for ZAPU, Muzorewa for the ANC, and Chikerema for Frolizi. On 8 December 1974, they signed a "unity" agreement to join together under the ANC. Muzorewa became chairman. This grouping broke up soon after. But one thing had changed after the talks between South Africa and Zambia. Vorster tried to show the African leaders that he was serious about the changes in Rhodesia. So he forced Smith to release the nationalist leaders who had been in detention for ten years. Mugabe, Nkomo, Sithole and others got out of prison.

Agents of Destruction

The Rhodesian Government still wanted to destroy ZANU and ZANLA. So some army officers tried to help some ZANLA commanders to take over the party. They held secret meetings in the bush near the Mozambique border. Then they took over the camp at Chifombo. They killed some other ZANLA guerrillas and kidnapped some of their leaders. This was called the Nhari Rebellion because it was led by Thomas Nhari. It ended when Tongogara went to the camp with loyal ZANLA forces and captured most of the rebels.

Then agents of the Rhodesian government murdered ZANU's national chairman, Herbert Chitepo. He had lived in Lusaka since 1966, leading the armed struggle. A bomb attached to his car exploded on 18 March 1975. It killed Chitepo, a bodyguard and a child in the next garden. The Zambian government arrested many ZANU leaders and ZANLA commanders, blaming them for Chitepo's murder.

Victoria Falls

The new ANC led by Bishop Muzorewa began talking to Smith. South Africa and Zambia tried to keep the talks going. In August 1975 Vorster crossed the Victoria Falls bridge to meet Kaunda in Zambia. They got Smith and the ANC leaders to meet in a railway train on the bridge. But Smith walked out after a few hours.

After the Victoria Falls meeting, the ANC leaders argued. Nkomo went home to Rhodesia. Muzorewa remained in exile. Both claimed to be the leader of the ANC.

"Protected Villages"

Smith did not want to talk about majority rule. He only wanted to talk about ending the fighting. So he did not need to talk in 1975 because there was very little fighting. There were two reasons for this. First, the Zambian government had detained many members of ZANU and ZANLA and put them in prison for almost two years. This meant that ZANLA guerrillas fighting in the north-east of Rhodesia could not get information or supplies of arms and ammunition. So they could not fight well.

The second reason why the war was slowing down was that the Smith government had begun to see that guerrillas moved among the people. So they began to move large numbers of people in the rural areas into what they called "protected villages". The Rhodesians said the guerrillas were forcing villagers to give them food and shelter. They said they were saving them by moving them inside fences and guarding them. But this was not true. Life inside these "protected villages" was very bad. The guerrillas called them **concentration camps**. They were crowded and the people living inside were always watched by the Rhodesian army. The Rhodesian army destroyed their old homes and even their crops and cattle to stop the guerrillas from having food and shelter.

President Nyerere of Tanzania and the new president of Mozambique, Samora Machel, agreed at first with Zambia's policy of talking to Smith and Vorster. But they soon saw that Smith would never accept majority rule unless the war forced him to do so. They had stopped giving military support to the guerrillas during detente. But after Mozambique independence in 1975, they began again to help ZANU and ZAPU to fight.

Journalists being shown around an early concentration camp or "protected village" where the people were forced to stay under Rhodesian army guard.

VOCABULARY

coup d'état	—	sudden action to change the governmnment by force.
officers	—	commanders in the army, air force or police.
dictators	—	rulers who keep power by force and not through the will of the people.
detente	—	when governments not friendly to each other try to improve their relations.
frontline	—	closest to, bordering on. This refers to the African countries bordering on the countries struggling for independence in Southern Africa.
concentration camps	—	places where large numbers of people are detained in very crowded, poor conditions.

EXERCISES

Summary

There was a *coup d'état* in _____ on 25 April _____. It was led by the Movement of the _____ _____. The new government soon gave independence to _____ _____ _____ and _____. This was a great help to the guerrillas fighting in _____ and _____. Zambia began talking to _____ _____. Some nationalist leaders were released from prison in _____ after _____ years. They met with others in Lusaka to talk about _____. Agents of the _____ government murdered ZANU's national Chairman _____ _____ in Lusaka on 18 March _____. They were trying to destroy _____.

Questions

1. How did the *coup d'état* in Portugal change things in Southern Africa?
2. Why was there little fighting in Rhodesia in 1975?
3. Why did the Rhodesian government move the people in rural areas into "protected villages"?

Discuss

Living together. How do events in one country affect people in another? How did the *coup d'état* in Portugal affect people in other countries? How did independence in Angola and Mozambique affect people in other countries?

Project
Watch for stories in the newspaper about Namibia and SWAPO. Namibia is not yet independent. SWAPO is fighting a liberation war there. Some members of the United Nations are trying to negotiate a settlement in Namibia. Namibia is meant to be protected by the United Nations. But it is occupied by South Africa. Clip these stories from the newspapers and bring them to school for discussion. If you hear a story on the radio about Namibia or SWAPO write it down and bring it to school.

President Machel led Frelimo to independence in Mozambique. But he said Mozambique would not be truly free until the rest of Southern Africa is free. The Frontline States are now helping SWAPO to get independence in Namibia.

23 The War Resumes

Smith announced a "**ceasefire**" after the Lusaka meeting of African leaders. That means both sides were meant to stop fighting. But the Rhodesian army continued to chase the guerrillas, and to drop papers from airplanes telling them to stop fighting. The ZANU leaders knew this was a trick. So they sent a paper to members that said they were not fighting to get Smith to talk, they were fighitng for majority rule. This meant that they should not stop fighting when Smith said he would talk, because they knew he would not talk about majority rule.

More Recruiting

Mugabe, Maurice Nyagumbo, Edgar Tekere and others had been released from detention. Now they returned home and began recruiting more people to join the war. It was much easier now that people all over the country had heard of the fighting in the north-east. They had heard of the courage of commanders like James Bond and Mao. Those were not real names. They were *chimurenga* names chosen to hide their identity so the Smith **regime** could not harm their relatives.

Mozambique independence was near and new recruits began to cross the border in large numbers. Then Chitepo was killed and there was not a senior ZANU leader outside the country to direct the war. The **central committee** met and decided that Mugabe and Tekere should go out to lead the recruits. Chief Tangwena helped them cross the border into Mozambique.

Leader Suspended

The frontline African presidents thought Sithole was still the leader of ZANU. They did not know he had been suspended by the other members of the central committee. The other ZANU leaders got very angry with him in 1969 when he said in court that he did not believe in violence or the armed struggle. The other ZANU leaders said he had **betrayed** the people who were fighting and those who had died. Then Sithole told the Rhodesian police he would talk to the other ZANU leaders about stopping the war. He thought if he said this the police would let him out of prison. But the police arranged a meeting for Sithole with other leaders in prison. They told him to finish his prison sentence and support the armed struggle.

Sithole continued to meet police officers. The other ZANU leaders in detention finally decided he should be suspended as president. This was in November 1974. One month later the nationalist leaders were allowed to go to the Lusaka meeting. So the ZANU leaders agreed to let Sithole act as president for a while longer to keep party unity. But a few months later he made them angry again. He did not try to find the truth about

People all over the country had heard of the fighting in the north-east. Recruits began to cross the border to Mozambique in large numbers.

Maurice Nyagumbo, the organizing secretary of ZANU, spent more than 20 years in detention and prison.

the murder of Chitepo. He accepted the detention of the ZANLA commanders by the Zambian government. He tried to make some of his friends the new commanders instead of Tongogara and others who were in detention. A few months later, Zambian soldiers shot and killed 11 ZANLA members detained at Mboroma camp. They wounded 13 others. Sithole did not go to the camp to find out what happened. He left the country. So the ZANLA commanders and members of the *Dare* detained in Zambia also decided Sithole could not remain as ZANU president.

Mgagao Declaration

The ZANLA commanders at Mgagao training camp in Tanzania made the same decision. They sent people to meet secretly with the leaders detained in Zambia. Soon after the Mboroma shooting in September 1975, the ZANLA guerrillas in Tanzania wrote one of the most important papers of the struggle. It was called the Mgagao Declaration. It **criticized** all of the main nationalist leaders except Mugabe. It said he was the only leader the guerrillas would accept. The Mgagao Declaration formally ended the role of Sithole as president. He kept on saying for several years that he was still the president. But the ZANLA guerrillas and most ZANU members no longer accepted this.

Mugabe Takes Over

Takawira had been the vice-president of ZANU. He died in prison in June 1970 when he was refused treatment for an illness. So the most senior leader was Mugabe, the secretary-general. He had taught others in detention and had studied hard himself. He had learned many things about law, education and administration. He passed three more university degrees while he was in detention. He was known for his honesty and commitment to the struggle. Mugabe was in Mozambique when the Mgagao Declaration was written. He was with the new recruits who were pouring across the border ready to fight. The last words of the Mgagao paper show how strongly the guerrillas felt about continuing the war. The paper said they would fight with stones if they had to: "If we cannot live as free men, we rather choose to die as FREE MEN."

ZIPA

During this time, there had been secret meetings at Mpima Prison in Zambia between the detained *Dare* members Tongogara, Kangai and others, and the ZAPU leaders Moyo and Silundika. They all wanted to get the war going again. They needed OAU help to do this, and the OAU said they must be united. They wanted to infiltrate through Mozambique, and Mozambique said they must be united. So they formed a new fighting force called the Zimbabwe People's Army (ZIPA). Nine commanders from ZANLA and nine from the ZAPU army, ZIPRA, formed

The commanders at Mgagao training camp in Tanzania signed a declaration saying Mugabe was the only leader they would accept.

Rex Nhongo, the chief of operations of ZANLA, became ZIPA commander.

Alfred "Nikita" Mangena, the ZIPRA commader, became political commissar and second-in-command.

a military committee. Rex Nhongo of ZANLA was the commander of ZIPA. Alfred "Nikita" Mangena of ZIPRA was the second-in-command.

New Offensive

On 17 January 1976, ZIPA resumed the war, this time on three fronts — Gaza, Manica and Tete. These were the names of provinces in Mozambique where the guerrillas had rear bases. This new **offensive** started the war again. There were attacks in many parts of the country. But the ZIPA command lasted only a few months. ZANLA and ZIPRA had different ways of approaching the struggle. ZANLA wanted to organize the people inside the country for guerrilla warfare. ZIPRA wanted to recruit more people to go out and prepare for regular warfare. Both wanted independence for Zimbabwe. The ZIPA period brought ZIPRA back into the war again after several years of training fighters in Angola, Tanzania, the Soviet Union and Zambia. In the ZIPA period, they were mostly recruiting. It was ZANLA who kept the ZIPA offensive going later in the year. Another problem was that Nkomo was talking to Smith. ZAPU members thought there might be an agreement soon. So they did not want to fight.

As we have seen in earlier chapters, the fighting again led to more talking. This time the United States of America joined Britain and South Africa in trying to stop the war.

VOCABULARY

ceasefire	—	a truce in a war when both sides agree to stop shooting.
regime	—	all parts of a government including the police and the army.
central committee	—	a group of leaders of the party.
betrayed	—	gave up on them, was disloyal, sold out.
criticized	—	said what was wrong with something or someone.
offensive	—	a series of attacks.

EXERCISES

Summary

The ZANU leaders knew _____ would not talk about _____ _____. So they had to keep on fighting until they got _____ _____. They returned home and began _____ more people to join the war. People had heard of the fighting in the north-east and the _____ of commanders like _____ _____ and _____. _____ independence was near and the _____ began to cross the border in large numbers. Then _____ died and there was not a senior political leader to outside to direct the war. The central committee decided that _____ and _____ should go out to lead the recruits. Chief _____ helped them cross the border to _____.

Questions

1. How did Sithole anger the ZANU leaders in detention in Rhodesia, in detention in Zambia, and in training camps in Tanzania?
2. What was the Mgagao Declaration and what did it say?
3. What was ZIPA and how did it resume the war?

Discuss

Prisons. Why do some people go to prison? There are small crimes such as stealing something, or big crimes such as killing someone. There are crimes against the government, such as trying to overthrow it. Nationalist leaders spent many years in prison, as we have seen. That was for political activity against the RF government, not for crimes. Nyagumbo spent more than 20 years in prison. Others were there for 10, 12 or 13 years. We have seen that the ZANU vice-president, Takawira, died in prison because he was not given treatment when he was sick. Why is it wrong to treat prisoners this way? How should prisoners be treated? Why should prisoners have books and magazines? How can we help prisoners to study, to teach others, and to improve their lives?

The Liberation War, 1976-77

Legend:
- ⬅ 1976 ZIPA Offensive on three fronts Tete, Manica and Gaza Provinces in Mozambique
- ⇦ Refugee routes to Mozambique, Zambia and Botswana
- ⬅ Rhodesian Forces' attacks on refugee camps in Zambia and Mozambique

Project

Education was something the people of Zimbabwe fought and died for. We have seen that most people were not allowed an education in the past. Education was a privilege, not a right. Now that we are in school, we have a duty to share our knowledge with those who were not allowed to learn. Many people in Zimbabwe still cannot read or write. They are illiterate. Identify some illiterate people in your community and spend a little of your time helping them learn to read and write.

Map shows: Malawi, Lake Niassa, Mkushi, Mumbwa, Freedom Camp, Lusaka, Zambia, Lake Cabora Bassa, Tete Province, Mozambique, Lake Kariba, Zambezi River, Harare, Manica Province, Nyadzonia, Mutare, Chimoio, Gondola, Rhodesia, Beira, Indian Ocean, Bulawayo, Gaza Province, Botswana, Limpopo River

24 The Patriotic Front

ZANU and ZAPU both wanted independence for Zimbabwe. So they worked together against the enemy. They formed the Joint Military Command in 1972. They formed ZIPA in 1975. Then in 1976, they formed a political partnership called the **Patriotic** Front.

Kissinger

The MPLA pushed the South African army out of southern Angola in early 1976. The South Africans were trying to put into power a **puppet** movement called UNITA. The American government also gave help to Unita and to another small group called the FNLA. They did not want the MPLA to win the colonial war. They were not sure the MPLA would allow western companies to continue to exploit the oil and diamonds there. So the USA began to look at what was going on in Southern Africa. After ZIPA started fighting in early 1976, the American government sent a powerful official to Southern Africa. He was the Secretary of State (Foreign Minister), Henry Kissinger.

Kissinger wanted to stop the nationalists from coming to power in Rhodesia. His government was worried that a **revolutionary** government might not allow American companies to exploit the resources. But he knew there had to be some changes. He knew that if the RF remained in power the guerrillas would continue to fight. They would become more revolutionary. He thought he could stop them by getting some small changes.

Henry Kissinger.

Machel

President Machel of Mozambique said the armed struggle was like a secondary school where students learned to fight for majority rule. Machel said that if the struggle continued the people would want more changes. They would want a socialist way of life where the wealth of the country was shared among all its people. They would not want a capitalist way of life where a few people get very rich while most people remain poor. He said that Kissinger was coming to close this "school" before the people learned about socialism.

"Not in a 1 000 Years"

Most people did not think Kissinger would get an agreement. Many other people had tried and failed. The nationalists knew Kissinger was trying to stop them from coming to power. So they did not trust him. Smith would not talk about majority rule. Three months of talks between Nkomo and Smith had broken down in March 1976. Kissinger arrived the next month, in April. Smith had said: "I don't believe in black majority rule ever in Rhodesia, not in a thousand years." So it did not seem likely that Kissinger would get Smith and the nationalists to agree.

Kissinger returned to Africa in September. He was in a stronger position. He knew more about the politics of Southern Africa. He had a powerful partner, South African Prime Minister Vorster. Kissinger and Vorster had decided that they could prevent a revolutionary government by getting Smith to accept majority rule. They could then put into power a **conservative** black government which would welcome relations with capitalist countries.

Just before Kissinger and Vorster met in September something else happened in the war. On 9 August 1976, the Rhodesian army attacked a **refugee** camp in Mozambique. This was at Nyadzonya. More than 1 000 unarmed Zimbabwe refugees were killed or wounded. Kissinger and Vorster saw that the war would soon spread to other countries in Southern Africa. So they put a lot of pressure on Smith to accept majority rule and end the war.

Hundreds of schoolchildren died when the enemy attacked Nyadzonya on 9 August 1976.

Smith Gives In

There was a meeting in South Africa that lasted for eight hours. Kissinger explained to Smith that Rhodesia was a very small part of the world. He said the American government would not support Rhodesia. The South African government applied economic pressure to get Smith to do what they wanted. They held back supplies of oil and weapons.

So on 24 September 1976, Smith made a broadcast on Rhodesian radio. He said he accepted majority rule, but the army, the police and other important areas must remain under white control. This was not what the nationalists meant by majority rule. This meant that power would remain with the white minority. Kissinger had not discussed this plan with the nationalist leaders. He talked only to Smith, Vorster and a few African presidents.

Geneva Conference

ZANU and ZAPU both said the agreement between Kissinger and Smith was wrong. But Kissinger had already organized a conference at the end of October 1976 in Geneva, Switzerland. The frontline African presidents said all nationalist leaders must attend.

This was when ZANU and ZAPU formed the Patriotic Front, so they could cooperate at the negotiations. A British **diplomat**, Ivor Richard, was chairman of the conference in Geneva. The talks went on for more than eight weeks. But there could be no agreement because Smith still did not want majority rule. Smith sent papers to the RF leaders at home. The papers said he would not agree to anything except an independent Rhodesia (not Zimbabwe) and an end to sanctions. Then the economy would improve. He could buy more guns to fight against the guerrillas.

David Owen.

Andrew Young.

The settlers agreed with this because Smith had used the radio, television, and newspapers to make them believe that the guerrillas were bad and must be killed.

The military activity in Rhodesia continued during the Geneva Conference. But there were problems in ZIPA. So there were not as many attacks as earlier in the year. This was also the time that a special unit of the Rhodesian army, called the Selous Scouts, began to kill missionaries. They tried to make it look like the guerrillas were killing the missionaries. They did not like the missionaries because many of them were giving food and medicine to the guerrillas.

There was an election in the USA in November 1976. Kissinger's government lost the election. Then Smith knew that Kissinger could no longer force him to accept an agreement. Kissinger had failed. But three important things had happened. Smith had accepted the idea of majority rule. He could no longer say there could never be a black government. Second, the ZANU and ZANLA leaders had been released from detention in Zambia for the Geneva talks. They went to Mozambique to resume the war. Third, the failure of the Geneva Conference had proved to many people that Smith would not accept change unless he was forced to.

Owen and Young

Then the British government and the new American government sent envoys to try to stop the war. The British foreign secretary, David Owen, and the American diplomat, Andrew Young, made several trips to Southern Africa. They talked to Smith and Vorster. They talked to the frontline presidents. And, unlike Kissinger, they talked to the nationalist leaders of the Patriotic Front. By the middle of 1977, they had a plan. This was called the Anglo-American plan. But Smith did not want this because all adults in Rhodesia would be allowed to vote. The Patriotic Front leaders wanted an election to be watched by people from outside the country to see that the voting was free and fair. So no one said "no" to the proposals, but no one said "yes" either.

Refugees

Africans living in the rural areas were badly treated by the Rhodesian police and army. People in the villages were beaten to get information about the guerrillas. Often people were killed and their huts were burned. Many thousands of people were forced into "protected villages". Thousands of people ran away to Botswana, Mozambique and Zambia. Sometimes in one day as many as 100 refugees would cross the border. Some became guerrillas. Many did not. Many were too young or too old to fight.

The refugees lived in special camps. They had no money or jobs. But ZANU, ZAPU, the United Nations, friendly governments and support groups looked after them. So did the country where they were staying. The refugees built their own houses and grew some of their own food. They were given mealie meal, beans and sometimes dried fish. They were given seeds and hoes. But there were so many people and never enough food. They were given a few clothes, shoes and blankets, and basic health care. But some people got sick and died.

More than 50 000 refugees were schoolchildren. There were not very many books and pens. The children usually sat under trees with their teachers. ZANU and ZAPU had to arrange for their education as well as fighting the war.

Air Raids

The Rhodesians spread the war into other countries just as Kissinger and Vorster had feared. The Rhodesian army and air force killed thousands of refugees in Angola, Mozambique and Zambia. They often attacked the camps. They dropped bombs from airplanes and shot at people on the ground when they ran away. The Rhodesians said they were attacking guerrillas. Sometimes they did. But unarmed refugees including children were killed at Chimoio, Gondola, Nyadzonia and Tembue in Mozambique, and at Freedom Camp, Mkushi and Mumbwa in Zambia. Enemy agents sometimes put poison into food and clothing for the refugees. So the people had to be **vigilant**. Life was very hard for the refugees. But they often sang and danced in the camps because they knew their country would soon be free. Life was also very hard for the people inside the country. But they continued to fight because they knew they would win. About 30 000 people died so Zimbabwe could be free.

ZANU and ZAPU had to educate the children as well as fighting the war. The refugee children had many hardships and many lost their lives in enemy attacks in Mozambique and Zambia.

VOCABULARY

patriotic	—	loving your country, prepared to fight for it.
puppet	—	a leader controlled by someone else.
revolutionary	—	in favour of great changes.
conservative	—	wanting to keep things the way they are, against change.
refugee	—	person forced to run away from their home.
diplomat	—	person representing their country in negotiations with other countries.
vigilant	—	always keeping watch.

EXERCISES

Summary

_____ and _____ formed the _____ _____ Command in 1972. They formed _____ in 1975. In 1976, they formed a political partnership called the _____ _____. Three months of talks between _____ and Smith broke down in March _____. Smith said: "I don't believe in _____ _____ _____ ever in _____, not in a _____ years." But _____ and _____ did not want the war to spread so they forced Smith to accept. The Rhodesian army had just attacked refugees at _____. Other refugee camps were attacked later at _____ and _____ in Mozambique, _____ and _____ in Zambia.

Questions

1. Why did Kissinger come to Africa?
2. Why did the Geneva Conference fail to reach agreement?
3. Why did so many people leave the country and become refugees?

Discuss

Rehabilitation. Disabled people. Many people have lost an arm or a leg or their eyesight or their hearing. This may have happened during the war, or it may have happened through sickness. These are normal people like everybody else, except for this. Sometimes they will need help. But they do not like to be treated as if they are a different kind of people. How can we help disabled people in our society? in school? at work? in the street? at home? Year of the Disabled 1982.

Project

Learn more about socialism. You can do this by looking around you. We have seen in an earlier chapter that the production unit at your school is an example of cooperative agriculture. This is a socialist idea, where everyone works together to produce something for the benefit of all. If you are looking after chickens at your school then the same applies. If you are selling or trading the chickens or eggs for money or other goods to help all of you, then this is a socialist idea. If one person bought the chickens and paid you to look after them, then kept the profit made by selling eggs, that would be capitalism. That person put up the money or capital. He would make sure that he made more money than the people who did the work. The capitalist would earn more money than the workers. You may be able to get someone to come to your school and speak about socialism in Zimbabwe. Or your teacher may be able to find some books to read from.

Some members of the ZANU central committee led by Robert Mugabe, and some members of the ZANLA high command at a meeting in the bush near Chimoio in Mozambique.

25 Gukurahundi

After the 1976 Geneva Conference, the war spread faster. Tongogara returned to command the ZANLA forces. ZIPRA became more involved in the war. Guerrilla operations reached every corner of the country. Soon the cities were surrounded. In 1978 the ZANLA guerrillas blew up oil storage tanks in Harare. This cost the Smith government millions of dollars of damage. The press, radio and television were **censored** so people in Rhodesia would not know the truth about the war. They were told the Rhodesian army was winning. Africans in the rural areas learned what was happening by listening to outside radio stations from Angola, Egypt, Tanzania and Zambia. They listened to the Voice of Zimbabwe broadcasts from Mozambique. ZANU President Mugabe named 1978 the "Year of the People" and 1979 *Gore reGukurahundi,* the "Year of the People's Storm".

The People

The people asked the guerrillas a lot of questions. They wanted to know if there would be taxes after independence, and how many cattle they could keep. They asked about communism and socialism. They went to secret meetings at night, called *pungwes*. They sang songs and talked about the national grievances. They sent their children to join the fight for freedom. Often police came, or the army, and they punished the people in the villages for helping the guerrillas. They were beaten, and sometimes killed. Their cattle were shot and their huts burnt. Later, Rhodesian soldiers destroyed their crops to stop the guerrillas from having food. People were often shot going to their fields. The Rhodesian **propaganda** always said they were "caught in crossfire" between the army and the guerrillas. By 1979 **martial law** covered most of the country. So the Rhodesian soldiers could do anything they wanted to do. There were many **atrocities**. Some people just disappeared. One of them was Edson Sithole. He was arrested by the police in 1975. He was seen in prison until 1978 and then he was never seen again.

Schoolchildren passed information to the guerrillas and warned them when the enemy was coming. They acted as eyes and ears for the freedom fighters. These young boys and girls were called *mujibas* and *chimbwidos*. By the end of the war they were more than 100 000 and were old people as well as young. They used certain **signals** to pass information over many miles. One signal was driving the cattle up or down a hill. Then the guerrillas could see from many miles away that it was safe, or there was trouble.

ZANLA guerrillas blew up oil storage tanks in Harare in December 1978 and destroyed the regime's petrol reserves.

Edson Sithole was seen in prison until 1978 and then he disappeared.

Liberated Zones

There were "no-go" areas where the Rhodesian army did not go at night. There were areas which were partly liberated. In the north-east and some eastern areas where the war had been going for a long time, there were liberated zones. There the people planted their crops and began to set up their own administration, education and health care. The guerrilas had permanent bases there.

By 1978 some Rhodesian army commanders were admitting that they could not defeat the guerrillas. The war was costing the Rhodesian government more than one million dollars a day. They depended on South Africa for most of their military supplies. All white men of all ages were called up for active military duty or reserve. Women served in the reserves. This meant the settlers were spending less time on the farm, in the factory, or at the office. This was bad for the economy. The Rhodesians forced Africans to join the army to fight against their brothers and sisters. Many ran away to join the guerrillas instead.

No main road in the country was safe from attack. The cars drove in convoys under armed guard.

More Talking

Britain and the USA sent more envoys to negotiate. But Smith refused to accept African rule. He flew to Zambia secretly to meet President Kaunda and then Nkomo. Smith did this twice, in 1977 and 1978. This angered the other frontline presidents and the ZANU leaders of the Patriotic Front, who had not been told about it.

More Fighting

On 22 January 1977, Rhodesian agents sent a parcel bomb to Lusaka which killed the second vice-president of ZAPU, Jason Moyo. He was a very popular leader who favoured unity. He helped to set up the JMC, ZIPA and the Patriotic Front. The commander of ZIPRA, Alfred "Nikita" Mangena, was killed in Zambia in June 1978. His truck ran over a landmine planted by Rhodesian agents.

ZIPRA guerrillas had very modern weapons. They could shoot down airplanes. In September 1978, they shot down an Air Rhodesia Viscount near Kariba. They shot down another one in February 1979. They said they were aiming for military officers such as the Rhodesian commander, Peter Walls. Many people died in the plane crashes. This made the Rhodesians very angry and they sent their planes to bomb camps in Zambia.

Jason Moyo, second vice-president of ZAPU, was killed in Lusaka by Rhodesian agents who sent him a parcel bomb.

Puppet Rule

Smith tried everything to stop the nationalist leaders from coming to power. At the end of 1977 he found some old African nationalists who would still talk to him even though he was killing their people. On 3 March 1978, he signed an agreement with Muzorewa, Rev. Sithole, and

Chief Jeremiah Chirau. Chirau was one of the chiefs paid by the RF government. None of them had support among the guerrillas. They saw that the only way to get power was to talk to Smith. The guerrillas called them puppets because they were working with the enemy and Smith was telling them what to do. They formed a government with Smith. They called Muzorewa "prime minister". They called the country "Zimbabwe-Rhodesia". Smith said he was sharing power with Africans, but he was not. The army, police, air force, courts and civil service remained under white control. So Africans did not have political, military or economic power.

Puppet Elections

By this time ZANLA had almost 15 000 guerrillas spread across the country. Groups of ZANLA guerrillas were crossing from Mozambique in large groups of several hundred at a time. They were training people in the villages to use guns. ZIPRA had almost 1 000 guerrillas in the country and was becoming more active in the north and west. The Rhodesian army could not handle this. Many mercenaries came from western countries to help them. But they still could not stop the advance of the guerrillas.

Chirau, Muzorewa, Sithole and Smith tried all kinds of tricks to stop the war. They said there was a ceasefire. They dressed some people as guerrillas and said they had given themselves up. They started their own "private armies". These men were poorly trained and **ill-disciplined**. They fought among themselves. Most people did not accept any of this because they wanted real independence. They knew which were the true freedom fighters. The war grew bigger and bigger.

In April 1979, the puppet group held elections for parliament. The whites had 28 seats out of 100. This meant they could always prevent any changes which might give Africans real power. Almost 100 000 Rhodesian soldiers were called up for the elections. Many stood with guns where the people were voting. Many people were forced to go and vote. The elections were not free. ZANU and ZAPU refused to take part in the elections because the people were being cheated. Muzorewa got most of the seats in the puppet election so he said the election was fair. Sithole did not get very many seats. So he said it was not fair. They disagreed among themselves. This was another trick by Smith to try to prevent real majority rule. But he could not fool the people.

In liberated and semi-liberated zones in eastern Zimbabwe, the people planted their crops and began to set up a new administration.

Smith could still find people who would talk to him even though his regime was killing their people. Muzorewa, Chirau and Sithole signed an agreement with him in March 1978.

VOCABULARY

censored	—	information taken out that the government did not want people to see or know about.
propaganda	—	spreading information of a certain kind.
martial law	—	military rules and laws.
atrocities	—	especially cruel actions of hurting or killing.
signals	—	some kind of sign to pass on information.
ill-disciplined	—	without discipline, treating people roughly.

EXERCISES

Summary

_____ returned to command the ZANLA forces. _____ became more involved in the war. The war spread through the rural areas until the _____ were surrounded. The _____, _____ and newspapers told Rhodesians they were winning the war. But they were not. Some army commanders were admitting this in _____. Africans in the rural areas learned about what was happening from the guerrillas and from _____ _____ in many other countries. They listened to the _____ of Zimbabwe from _____. ZIPRA guerrillas shot down two Air Rhodesia _____. This made the Rhodesians very angry and they sent planes to bomb camps in _____. Even though their people were being killed, some Africans signed an agreement with Smith. They were _____, _____ and _____.

Questions

1. Who were the *mujibas* and *chimbwidos*? How did they help to free the country?
2. Who was Jason Moyo?
3. Why were Chirau, Muzorewa and Sithole called puppets?
4. Why did ZANU and ZAPU refuse to take part in the April 1979 elections?

Discuss

Reconstruction. The war went on for many years. Many buildings were destroyed. There were never enough schools, health clinics and other services in the rural areas. It will take us many years to build and rebuild. How can we help in the reconstruction of Zimbabwe?

Spread of the Liberation War

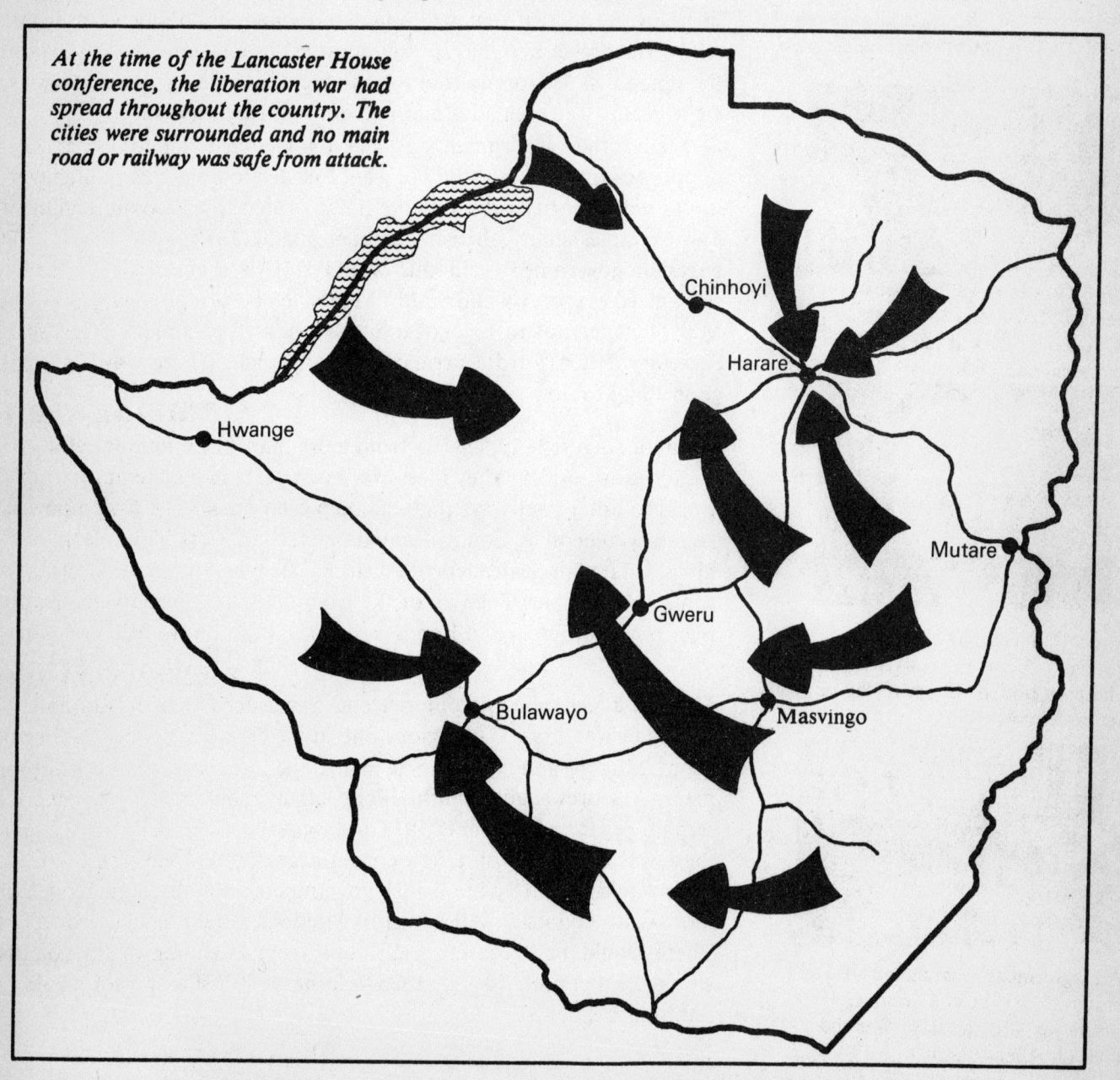

Project

Act out a *pungwe*. A few students can be freedom fighters. The rest are people in the village. Some of the people in the village can be *mujibas* and *chimbwidos*. They make up a signal to the guerrillas that it is safe to come. Then they chant slogans together and sing songs. The people in the village ask a lot of questions. They ask questions about what is happening in the war. They ask questions about what will happen when the war is over. Then maybe a *mujiba* or *chimbwido* on guard signals that the enemy is coming and everyone runs away. Make up your own play about a *pungwe*.

At the time of the Lancaster House conference, the liberation war had spread throughout the country. The cities were surrounded and no main road or railway was safe from attack.

26 The Birth of Zimbabwe

Members of the OAU and the United Nations refused to accept the Zimbabwe-Rhodesia elections and the puppet government. They said it was not majority rule.

Then there were elections in Britain and a new government came to power. The Conservative party won the elections. Margaret Thatcher became the British Prime Minister. This was in May 1979. Thatcher did not like the guerrillas. She called them "terrorists". African governments were worried that she would **recognize** Smith's new government when Muzorewa became "prime minister" on 1 June. Then she would lift sanctions. Muzorewa and Smith would be able to buy more guns to fight against the guerrillas and prevent real majority rule.

Many other governments asked Mrs Thatcher not to recognize the puppet government. She did not want to listen to political arguments that it was not majority rule. But she had to listen to economic arguments. For example, many British companies did business in Nigeria. The Nigerian government said this would stop if the British government recognized Muzorewa and Smith. Many members of her own party asked Mrs Thatcher not to recognize Smith's new government. Her Foreign Secretary, Peter (Lord) Carrington, finally made her see that it was not a good thing to do.

Commonwealth

Then, in August 1979, leaders from more than 40 **Commonwealth** countries met in Lusaka. They meet every two years in a different part of the world to talk about ways they can help each other. The Commonwealth secretary-general is Sonny Ramphal. He had worked out a plan. He discussed it with the leaders of Australia, Britain, Jamaica, Nigeria, Tanzania and Zambia. Then all of the Commonwealth leaders accepted the plan for a conference in London to discuss the future of Rhodesia.

Lancaster House

Mrs. Thatcher called a conference at Lancaster House in London. The chairman was Lord Carrington. She invited the leaders of the Patriotic Front, Mugabe and Nkomo. She invited the leaders of the puppet government, Muzorewa and Smith. Many other people went too. The conference began in September 1979 and went on for three months. Finally, there was agreement on a new constitution and new elections. The elections would be run by the British government with **observers** from Commonwealth countries. All adults in Rhodesia would be allowed to vote. There would be a ceasefire. Soldiers from Commonwealth countries would see that both sides stopped fighting. A British governor would rule until independence.

Margaret Thatcher became the British Prime Minister after the Conservative party won the election there.

The Commonwealth Secretary-General, Shridath (Sonny) Ramphal of Guyana, worked out a plan for a conference in London.

Lord Carrington, the British Foreign Secretary, advised Mrs. Thatcher not to recognize the puppet government.

An agreement was signed at Lancaster House on 21 December 1979, seven years to the day after the attack on Altena Farm.

The PF leaders did not like everything about the agreement. They did not like the racist constitution that reserved 20 out of 100 seats in parliament for the white minority. They did not like the fact that blacks and whites would vote separately. They thought everyone should vote together. But the agreement contained most of the important things they had been fighting for. It allowed every adult to vote. There would be majority rule and independence for Zimbabwe. So they accepted. The Lancaster House agreement was signed on 21 December 1979. This was seven years to the day after the attack on Altena Farm, the first attack of the decisive phase of the war.

Ceasefire

ZANLA and ZIPRA commanders flew into Harare on 26 December 1979. Crowds of people met them at the airport, shouting and singing. Fighting stopped on 28 December. They had only one week to get guerrillas all over the country into assembly points. The Rhodesians did not think the commanders could do it. They thought that after one week they could go and shoot the ones who had not come in. It was a credit to the commanders and the discipline of the guerrillas that by 5 January more than 17 000 had assembled at the chosen places. All sides kept their weapons in case of attack from the other side. Rhodesian soldiers were meant to be restricted to their bases, but they showed less discipline than the guerrillas. The private armies of the puppet leaders were the most ill-disciplined.

Mugabe and Nkomo returned in January 1980. The people organized huge rallies to celebrate. There was a lot of security because their lives were in danger. Many people inside and outside the country still wanted to stop majority rule. They tried to kill Mugabe. The South African government gave millions of dollars to other parties to try to stop ZANU from winning the election. The Rhodesian army unit, the Selous Scouts, planted bombs at churches in Harare. They tried to say it was done by ZANU. They said ZANU was against Christians. Other members of the Rhodesian army ambushed a bus near Rusape and killed 14 people. They tried to blame it on ZANLA and use it as an excuse to start the war again. The Rhodesians put lies in newspapers and other papers. They blew up the printing presses at Mambo Press in Gweru because the newspaper, *Moto,* was supporting the PF leaders.

1980 Elections

ZANU had to call itself ZANU(PF) because Sithole was saying he was the leader of ZANU. He was trying to confuse the people to vote for him. ZANU(PF) had to change its election **symbol** because the British election committee would not allow it to use a gun and a hoe. So it chose the cock, the *jongwe.* This was a very popular symbol and many people

There was a ceasefire in the war. The guerillas left the villages and moved into assembly points.

Lord Soames was the British governor during the transition.

waiting to vote were flapping their arms like a *jongwe*. When the British Governor, Lord Soames, saw this he knew that ZANU(PF) was going to win. He did not have good relations with ZANU(PF) and he had stopped members from making speeches in some areas.

The elections were held on 27 to 29 February 1980. Each party put up a list of people for each of the eight provinces. Then if they got 10 per cent of the votes in one province, the first names on their list would become members of parliament. The vote was secret. Each person went into a small booth where no one else could see. Each person marked an *X* on a small paper called a ballot. The *X* was put beside the symbol of the party they wanted to vote for.

The results were announced on 4 March 1980. The people had given ZANU(PF) a majority, with 57 seats in parliament. ZAPU won 20 seats. Muzorewa's ANC won three seats. The white election was held earlier. The Rhodesian Front won all 20 seats reserved for whites.

Transition

Many whites were frightened when ZANU(PF) won the election. Their radio, television and newspapers had been telling them lies. They thought Muzorewa would win. Walls, the army commander, even sent a message to Mrs Thatcher asking her not to accept the election results.

On the same night that the election results were announced, Mugabe made a broadcast on radio and television to all of the people of Zimbabwe. He talked about unity. He talked about working together to build Zimbabwe. He said everyone's rights would be safe. He had promised that ZANU(PF) would form a government with ZAPU. So Nkomo and other ZAPU leaders were invited to join the first government of Zimbabwe. He promised **reconciliation** after the war with the settlers. So he invited two whites to join the government. One of them was a member of the RF.

Independence

ZANU(PF) formed the people's government. Mugabe became the Prime Minister. He named a government of new ministers. ZANU(PF) also named a president because the Lancaster House constitution said they must have a separate head of state. Canaan Banana became the president. Zimbabwe became independent on 18 April 1980. There was a big ceremony at Rufaro Stadium in Harare at midnight the night before. Soldiers of ZANLA, ZIPRA and the Rhodesian army marched past. This was the beginning of the unified army of Zimbabwe. They all watched the new Zimbabwe flag raised to the top of the pole for the first time.

The most important guerrilla commander who had organized the new approach to the struggle was not present at Independence. Tongogara had died in a car accident in Mozambique on 26 December 1979, the

Mugabe returned to Harare on 27 January 1980 and was welcomed at a huge mass rally in Highfield.

Party election symbols. The people chose the *jongwe*.

Robert Gabriel Mugabe, first Prime Minister of Zimbabwe.

same day the other commanders flew to Harare. He was on his way to the ZANLA headquarters at Chimoio to tell the commanders of the agreement. He, and thousands of others who died in the liberation war, will always be remembered as **heroes** of the struggle for Zimbabwe.

The new Zimbabwe flag was raised at midnight on the eve of independence.

Josiah Tongogara: "We used to throw stones at each other in Harare. We cannot pass this on to our kids. We are going away and we must leave a stable Zimbabwe to the new generation."

VOCABULARY

recognize	—	accept the government and open diplomatic relations.
Commonwealth	—	loose organization of former British colonies in all parts of the world.
observers	—	people who watch carefully.
symbol	—	a sign that represents something.
reconciliation	—	accepting people with whom you have disagreed in the past.
heroes	—	people remembered for their courage and leadership.

EXERCISES

Summary

The _____ party won the elections in Britain and _____ _____ became the prime minister. The _____ government said it would stop business with Britain if it recognized the puppet government of _____ and _____. The leaders of more than 40 _____ countries met in _____ and agreed on a plan worked out by the secretary-general, _____ _____. There was a conference at _____ _____ in London. _____ was the chairman. It began in September _____. There was agreement on a new constitution and new _____. There was a _____ in the war. _____ won the most seats in the elections and _____ became the first prime minister of Zimbabwe.

Questions

1. What role did the Commonwealth play in Zimbabwe's independence?
2. What was the Lancaster House agreement?
3. How did some people inside and outside the country try to stop ZANU (PF) coming to power?
4. What did Mugabe say in his broadcast after the election results were announced?

Discuss

Each year Zimbabwe has several public holidays when people do not have to go to work or school. Some of these holidays are special days in honour of people who died in the war. Independence Day is 18 April. Workers Day is 1 May. Africa Day is 25 May. That is the day when the OAU was formed on 1963 to promote freedom and unity in Africa. Heroes Days are 9 and 10 August. Pause for a moment and think about all of the things you have read in this book. Think about the people who died in the war. They died so you could be free. They died so you could work hard to build a good future for yourself and your children. Discuss all these things with your friends and your family.

Project
Continue to learn about history in Zimbabwe and other countries. Zimbabwe history did not stop with independence. Zimbabwe is not the only country which struggled for freedom and independence. The struggle continues. We can learn from what happened in the past. We can learn to protect our freedom. We may have to fight again to keep it. We must remember that the people in South Africa are not yet free. We must be vigilant. We must be united.

The first government of Zimbabwe.

Other Books to Read:

Early History
D.N. Beach, *The Shona and Zimbabwe 900 — 1850*, Mambo Press, Gweru, 1980.
A. Chigwedere, *From Mutapa to Rhodes*, Macmillan, 1980.
P.S. Garlake, *Great Zimbabwe Described and Explained*, Zimbabwe Publishing House, Harare, 1982.
P.S. Garlake, *Life at Great Zimbabwe*, Mambo Press, Gweru, 1982.
S.I. Mudenge, *History of Munhumutapa*, Zimbabwe Publishing House, Harare, 1982.

19th Century
N. Bhebe, *Lobengula of Zimbabwe*, Heinemann Educational Books, London, 1977.
R.K. Rasmussen, *Mzilikazi of the Ndebele*, Heinemann Educational Books, London, 1977.
S. Samkange, *Origins of Rhodesia*, Heinemann Educational Books, London, 1968.

The First Chimurenga
T.O. Ranger, *Revolt in Southern Rhodesia 1896-7*, Heinemann Educational Books, London, 1967.

African Nationalism
S. Machel, *Sowing the Seeds of Revolution*, Zimbabwe Publishing House, Harare, 1981.
E. Mlambo, *The Struggle for a Birthright*, C. Hurst and Company, London, 1972.
M. Nyagumbo, *With the People*, The Graham Publishing Company, Harare, 1980.
T.O. Ranger, *The African Voice in Southern Rhodesia*, Zimbabwe Publishing House, Harare, forthcoming.
N. Shamuyarira, *Crisis in Rhodesia*, East African Publishing House in association with Andre Deutsch, 1967.
W. Smith, *Nyerere of Tanzania*, Zimbabwe Publishing House, Harare, 1981.

The Liberation War
Catholic Commission for Justice and Peace, *Civil War in Rhodesia*, Catholic Institute for International Relations, London, 1976.
C. Hove, *Up in Arms*, Zimbabwe Publishing House, Harare, 1982.
D. Martin and P. Johnson, *The Struggle for Zimbabwe· the Chimurenga War*, Zimbabwe Publishing House, Harare, 1981.
M. Raeburn, *Blackfire*, Mambo Press, Gweru, 1981.
T. Wigglesworth, *Perhaps Tomorrow*, Galaxie Press, Harare, 1981.

General
M. Bailey, *Oilgate*, Coronet Books, London, 1979.
R.G. Clarke, *Foreign Companies and International Investment in Zimbabwe*, Mambo Press, Gweru, 1980;
G. Kahari, *The Search for a Zimbabwean Identity*, Mambo Press, Gweru, 1980.
I. Linden, *The Catholic Church and the Struggle for Zimbabwe*, Longman, London, 1980.
M. Loney, *Rhodesia — White Racism and Imperial Response*, Penguin, London, 1975.
C. van Onselen, *Chibaro — African Mine Labour in Southern Rhodesia 1900 — 1933*, Ravan Press, Johannesburg, 1980.
R. Palmer, *Land and Racial Domination in Rhodesia*, Heinemann Educational Books, London, 1977.
Q.N. Parsons and R. Palmer, *Roots of Rural Poverty in Central and Southern Africa*, University of California Press, 1977.
Q.N. Parsons, *A New History of Southern Africa*, Macmillan (Boleswa), London, 1982.
W. Rodney, *How Europe Underdeveloped Africa*, Zimbabwe Publishing House, Harare, 1981.